"I hope that every youth ministry leader reads *Faith Beyond Youth Group*. This book not only locates where young people are at but provides insightful, practical, and doable ways to truly cultivate lifelong discipleship. This book is for all youth ministry leaders regardless of the size or context of their youth ministry. It's not a one-size-fits-all approach to youth ministry; it's an approach that values and esteems every young person entrusted to you by God. It is hope-filled and provides a way forward for discipling young people in these rapidly changing times."

Christine Caine, founder of A21 and Propel Women

"I genuinely want the teenagers I work with to develop Christlike character. (I desire this in my own life as well.) But that's not because I want them to be good girls and boys who grow up to be well-behaved church members; my motivation is that I want teenagers to experience vitality and a glorious partnership with Jesus in his redemptive work in the world. *Faith Beyond Youth Group* provides rails to run on with research, theological insight, and plenty of practical ideas, bringing to life what some might wrongly think of as a rusty relic of the past."

Mark Oestreicher, founder and partner, The Youth Cartel

"The church is facing a crisis of disintegration. Too many Christians have been formed to dis-integrate their spiritual life with Christ from their life at work, school, and the public square. As a result, the way of Jesus may inform how they conduct their private relationships or manage their households but may not be carried into the more public or communal parts of their lives. Unfortunately, this has severely damaged the witness of the church and the reputation of the faith—particularly among the young. How can we avoid making the same mistake with a new generation? Rooted in research and data, *Faith Beyond Youth Group* reimagines what youth ministry can look like if our goal isn't behavior management but rather character formation. It presents a vision of youth ministry that isn't primarily about disintegrated events but rather teaching, practices, and relationships that occur throughout a young person's life. There is wisdom here for every church that cares about the next generation."

Skye Jethani, author of *What If Jesus Was Serious?* and cohost of *The Holy Post* podcast

"*Faith Beyond Youth Group* is a game-changing resource for those in youth ministry. Kara Powell, Brad M. Griffin, and Jen Bradbury present new research along with stories from their ministry experiences to offer a practical tool for youth workers. The book provides effective ideas and insightful reflection questions to help readers chart their map forward, empowering them to help young people move beyond the traditional youth group experience with a rooted, sustainable life of faith. If you're a youth worker who wants to significantly impact young people's spiritual development, this book is a must-have resource."

Christina Lamas, executive director, National Federation for Catholic Youth Ministry

"This book had me at the title: *Faith Beyond Youth Group*. It's what we all want, hope, and pray for—faith that matters long after our games, teaching, camps, and programs are over. Even better, the book delivers a clear and hopeful compass to reorient youth ministry toward what matters most."

Doug Fields, youth pastor and president of DownloadYouthMinistry.com

"Every discipline has a set of standards. Youth ministry is no exception. *Faith Beyond Youth Group* addresses the questions youth leaders ask themselves regarding their impact on the youth they love and willingly serve. The authors include interviews and stories from various youth leaders, highlighting their journey of discipling young people who attend youth group. The theological insights walk the reader through a process of understanding the benefits and barriers of character formation. This book is an informative, reflective, and practical approach for youth leaders to follow while they assess lifelong discipleship beyond youth group. This is a welcomed addition to the library of every youth leader."

Virginia Ward, Gordon-Conwell Theological Seminary, Boston Campus

"*Faith Beyond Youth Group* is a must read for anyone invested in deepening Gen Z's faith. Each chapter combines Fuller Youth Institute's meticulous research with inspiring and thought-provoking stories about local youth workers in the trenches. These stories model a great deal of humility toward the next generation, and they offer so many practical tools to help us work within our various local church contexts. As someone coming from an Asian American youth ministry experience, I was impressed to see how much care and depth they put into making sure that we didn't feel overwhelmed or excluded from the conversation around the state of the Gen Z's faith; rather, I was encouraged to see how we could learn from many different cultural and socioeconomic perspectives."

Kevin Yi, college and young adults pastor at Church Everyday, CA

FAITH
BEYOND
YOUTH
GROUP

Previous Books by Authors

Growing Young by Kara Powell, Jake Mulder, and Brad Griffin

Growing With by Kara Powell and Steven Argue

3 Big Questions That Change Every Teenager
by Kara Powell and Brad M. Griffin

3 Big Questions That Shape Your Future by Kara Powell,
Kristel Acevedo, and Brad M. Griffin

FIVE WAYS TO FORM CHARACTER AND
CULTIVATE LIFELONG DISCIPLESHIP

FAITH
BEYOND
YOUTH
GROUP

KARA POWELL, JEN BRADBURY, AND
BRAD M. GRIFFIN

BakerBooks
a division of Baker Publishing Group
Grand Rapids, Michigan

Published by Baker Books
a division of Baker Publishing Group
Grand Rapids, Michigan
www.bakerbooks.com

Printed in the United States of America

Library of Congress Cataloging-in-Publication Data
Names: Powell, Kara Eckmann, 1970– author. | Bradbury, Jen, 1980– author.|
    Griffin, Brad M., 1976– author.
Title: Faith beyond youth group : five ways to form character and cultivate lifelong
    discipleship / Kara Powell, Jen Bradbury, and Brad M. Griffin.
Description: Grand Rapids, Michigan : Baker Books, a division of Baker Publishing
    Group, [2023] | Includes bibliographical references. |
Identifiers: LCCN 2023002259 | ISBN 9781540903518 (cloth) | ISBN 9781493443338
    (ebook)
Subjects: LCSH: Personality development. | Youth development. | Leadership.
Classification: LCC BF723.P4 P68 2023 | DDC 259/.23—dc23/eng/20230512
LC record available at https://lccn.loc.gov/2023002259

Unless otherwise indicated, Scripture quotations are from THE HOLY BIBLE, NEW INTERNATIONAL VERSION®, NIV® Copyright © 1973, 1978, 1984, 2011 by Biblica, Inc.® Used by permission. All rights reserved worldwide.

Scripture quotations labeled NASB are from the (NASB®) New American Standard Bible®, Copyright © 1960, 1971, 1977, 1995, 2020 by The Lockman Foundation. Used by permission. All rights reserved. www.lockman.org

This project was made possible through the support of a grant from the John Templeton Foundation. The opinions expressed in this publication are those of the authors and do not necessarily reflect the views of the John Templeton Foundation.

The names and details of the people and situations described in this book have been changed or presented in composite form in order to ensure the privacy of those with whom the authors have worked.

The authors are represented by WordServe Literary Group, www.wordserveliterary .com.

Baker Publishing Group publications use paper produced from sustainable forestry practices and post-consumer waste whenever possible.

23 24 25 26 27 28 29   7 6 5 4 3 2 1

This book is dedicated to our ministry mentors who embodied deep character, giving us living pictures of Faith Beyond Youth Group:

Mike and Kristi DeVito
Kitty Ganzel
Hal Hamilton

Contents

ONE

CHARACTER

More Than an Outdated Catchphrase

"'We just have to make it to Friday night youth group.' That's what the girls in my small group text each other. And me."

That was how one small group leader described the youth group's impact on the eleventh-grade girls she mentored. The other five volunteers sitting on folding chairs in the center of the youth room nodded in agreement.

I (Kara) could see why this youth group was a refuge. During our research team's site visit, I sensed it too. The worship music was simple, but the student musicians seemed sincere and passionate about their relationship with Jesus. The youth pastor didn't talk *at* the kids but *with* the kids, authentically discussing the highs and lows of his faith journey. There was ample time to process afterward in small groups led by an ethnically diverse volunteer team. The groups often ran past their designated end time—a good sign of deepening community. Students showed up early and stayed late because they wanted to be with each other and the adults who poured into them week after week.

This youth pastor and volunteer team were proud of how much students loved their Friday nights together. And rightly so. The spiritual oasis they'd created inspired our team of researchers—all of whom are current or past youth leaders. But then we started to wonder, *What about the rest of the week?*

Our question echoes those we've heard from youth leaders like you . . .

- How does what we teach teenagers actually improve their lives and the lives of those around them?
- What do we do in our ministries that truly forms the faith of students?
- How can we measure the effectiveness of youth discipleship?
- Why do so many students act one way in youth group and another everywhere else? How can we close that gap?
- How can we help students understand that following Jesus is more about being "for" what is good than being "against" certain elements of culture?
- How can we do any of this well when we get so little time with students in our ministries and communities?

By "youth group," we mean the teenagers in your youth ministry, your weekly gathering, and/or an umbrella term for your youth ministry. Since different leaders and faith traditions use some or all of these definitions, we likewise do the same.

Whether your youth group meets for forty-five minutes on Sunday mornings, two hours on Sunday nights, ninety minutes on Wednesdays, or five hours on Friday evenings, that's only a small fraction of a young person's week. *How do teenagers fare the other days? And not just the rest of their week but the rest of their lives?*

If you're like us, you want kids to not only feel different during youth group but also *be* different both before and after.

Unfortunately, it's not clear that youth group as we know it makes an immediate or lasting difference. Regular participation in religious services lowers rates of teenage depression and drug usage and raises levels of academic achievement, happiness, and forgiveness.[1] But it's also been found to decrease young people's sense of overall well-being and the quality of their parental relationships.[2]

While spiritual and religious activity under age eighteen seems to slightly increase the odds of faith lasting after youth group,[3] a compilation of studies indicates that about 40 to 50 percent of youth group kids drift from God and the faith community after graduation.[4]

In the longer term, adults who attended church as a child are twice as likely to read the Bible and 50 percent more likely to pray during a typical week as those who didn't. But that same study found that adults who were churched as young people had similar beliefs as adults who grew up unchurched.[5]

When we combine this information with estimates that over one million teenagers leave the faith annually,[6] it's easy to get discouraged. It's also understandable that we hear so many leaders say they want to quit.

Approximately 42 percent of full-time US pastors have considered quitting ministry in the last year.[7] In a parallel study of full-time youth leaders, that figure hovered at a similar 41 percent.[8] Given this widespread pastoral discouragement, we can't help but wonder if in addition to the pressures of the pandemic, political division, racial unrest, economic struggles, and church conflict, there's another reason so many leaders feel like throwing in the towel.

When we feel burned out, it may be because we're working too much. But one recent employment study indicates that while burnout may be due to too much work, it's often also the result of *too little impact*.[9]

Did you catch that?

Burnout happens when we feel like our work doesn't matter.

There's not a youth leader among us who hasn't felt this way, particularly on the heels of having to constantly pivot as our world and young people continue to change. In fact, it feels like every time we meet with youth leaders, we hear them say things like,

> "We definitely have some amazing students, but so many others are spiritually lethargic."
>
> "I'm working more than ever, and it's not making a difference."
>
> "I'm so tired."
>
> "None of my kids come anymore."
>
> "No one cares about what I'm doing."

No wonder we're all exhausted.

We see you.

We hear you say you're doing everything you know how to do to minister to young people.

We agree it's not working.

That's because if teenagers' faith is just a youth group faith, it's too small to captivate their entire week . . . let alone their entire lives. What teenagers need is a relationship with Jesus that changes not just ninety minutes of their week but 100 percent of their lives.

To unwrap young people's full potential, maybe it's time we reorient our focus to one game-changing gift: *character.*

Rediscovering Character in Scripture

Character can be a loaded term. For some of us, the word is filled with baggage because of how it has been used to get us to conform to a certain set of standards. It's inseparably tied to morality. For others, character feels dated, like something that was valued in a bygone era by our grandparents but is not necessary now. Others of us might primarily associate character with elementary school curriculum that tries to instill qualities like honesty, forgiveness, and resilience in kids.

Still others might associate character with a set of spiritual rules to follow and behaviors to avoid. When we come from traditions that emphasize purity, holiness, piety, or other versions of strict norms that feel more like control than "freedom in Christ," it's understandable that mentions of character can make us bristle.

Based on a comprehensive review of character from Scripture, our research team defines *character* as:

Living out Jesus' goodness every day by loving God and our neighbors.

When we say "our team" and "our research team," we're referring to the incredible staff at the Fuller Youth Institute (FYI), where we serve alongside committed team members who care deeply about turning research into resources that equip adults who influence young people to live faithfully. FYI is also the backbone organization for TENx10, a national collaboration that seeks to make faith matter more for ten million young people over the next ten years, in the spirit of John 10:10. To find out more, visit FullerYouth Institute.org and TENx10.org.

We believe we can rediscover how Scripture keeps character and faith integrated rather than either obsessing over rules or separating spirituality from the rest of life. If faith is what is believed, then character is faith lived out in real time.

Character in the Old and New Testaments

From the earliest verses of the Old Testament, it is clear that God values character. Despite their flaws, our early Bible protagonists are often recognized for their flashes of character.

In a time of wickedness, Noah finds favor in the eyes of God and is saved from the flood because of his righteousness.

When God chooses David—a leader who later uses his power egregiously—God tells Samuel, "The LORD does not look at the things people look at. People look at the outward appearance, but the LORD looks at the heart" (1 Sam. 16:7).

As a young person herself, Esther courageously steps forward to advocate for her Jewish people during the Persian diaspora "for such a time as this" (Esther 4:14).

In the New Testament, when God becomes incarnate and chooses to live among us, Jesus embodies God's character. Jesus models character for his followers and teaches explicitly about character on multiple occasions, perhaps most famously in the Sermon on the Mount, when Jesus calls his followers to live according to the future kingdom in the present world.

From the earliest days of Jesus' ministry, love is what marks his followers. In John 13:35, Jesus teaches, "By this everyone will know that you are my disciples, if you love one another." Of all the options Jesus could use as the metric for his success, he chooses love—a virtue. He spends three years loving his disciples and teaching them how to do the same.

By focusing on character, Jesus instills his discipleship DNA in his friends. His identity shapes theirs. By forming a community with his twelve closest apostles, he gives his followers a place to belong that reinforces the character he is forming in them. He then sends them out into the world with a clear mission to do what he did—to love God and others and, through that love, make disciples.

Only one out of Jesus' twelve apostles leaves the community he formed. The eleven apostles who stay, plus a number of other men and women close to Jesus, consistently demonstrate their character and faith throughout their daily lives.

The New Testament epistles also wrestle with how the early church should live—and so much of this is about character.

We also glory in our sufferings, because we know that suffering produces perseverance; perseverance, character; and character, hope. And hope does not put us to shame, because God's love has been poured out into our hearts through the Holy Spirit, who has been given to us. (Rom. 5:3–5)

But the fruit of the Spirit is love, joy, peace, forbearance, kindness, goodness, faithfulness, gentleness and self-control. Against such things there is no law. Those who belong to Christ Jesus have crucified the flesh with its passions and desires. Since we live by the Spirit, let us keep in step with the Spirit. (Gal. 5:22–25)

Therefore, as God's chosen people, holy and dearly loved, clothe yourselves with compassion, kindness, humility, gentleness and patience. Bear with each other and forgive one another if any of you has a grievance against someone. Forgive as the Lord forgave you. And over all these virtues put on love, which binds them all together in perfect unity. (Col. 3:12–14)

Make every effort to live in peace with everyone and to be holy; without holiness no one will see the Lord. (Heb. 12:14)

Across the Scriptures, character lies at the core of being Christian.

Talking about Character Today

Many of us look not only to Scripture but also to other wise voices to understand character. Here are some of the ways others have described character as well as *virtue*, a word often used to describe specific character qualities.

"In justice is summed up the whole of virtue." —Aristotle[10]

"[Character is] a set of dispositions, desires, and habits that are slowly engraved during the struggle against your own weakness." —David Brooks[11]

"[Character is] choosing what is loving and right, cultivating the habits of virtue so that they may become natural, or second nature." —Amy Peterson[12]

"[Character is] the pattern of thinking and acting which runs right through someone, so that wherever you cut into them (as it were), you see the same person through and through." —N. T. Wright[13]

"Character is revealed in how well we love." —Rich Villodas[14]

How do today's teenagers describe character? One diverse group of students landed on "How you describe yourself" and "Who you are . . . mostly." We thought the inclusion of "mostly" was particularly insightful, because these young people recognized that none of us are consistent everywhere all the time.

A seventeen-year-old young woman reflected, "Character is who someone is deep down, the way that they treat other people, and the way that they carry themselves." And an eighteen-year-old young man summed up, "Simply put, character is the thing that separates you from a stereotype." He went on to share, "I think character can often be overlooked, because people don't see the other parts of someone outside their stereotype. I do think that there are people who present their character more. It takes bravery not to hide within a stereotype. People don't develop character as much as they learn to let people, including themselves, see it more."

Is Forming Character the Same as Forming "Good Kids"?

To be clear, forming character is not about trying to manipulate young people into behaving a certain way so that they can earn God's love (or ours!). It's also not about trying to form "good kids," an expression we're quite confident you've heard before—likely at your own church.

In one congregation I (Jen) served, our high schoolers led worship every year on Youth Sunday. At the end of Youth Sunday, parishioners would inevitably tell me, "We have such good kids."

They were right. We had *good* kids.

The problem is the goal of Christian formation isn't just to make good kids. It's to form disciples with the character of Christ. While good kids and disciples with Christlike character are related, they aren't the same.

Good kids are generally nice people, particularly when they're on display.[15] Teenagers with Christlike character do the right thing even when no one is watching.

Good kids don't question what grown-ups in their lives expect. Teenagers with Christlike character sometimes question (or even defy) others' expectations in order to live out Jesus' command to love God and others.

Good kids don't bully others. Teenagers with Christlike character confront bullies. Like Jesus, they use their voices to advocate for those on the margins.

Good kids get involved in causes because they long to make the world a better place (while also beefing up their college résumés). Teenagers with Christlike character get involved in causes because that's what following Jesus compels them to do (whether or not it looks good on their college résumés).

Good kids stay out of trouble. Teenagers with Christlike character sometimes get into "good trouble," the kind of holy trouble Jesus made when he confronted powerful people and systems of oppression.[16]

Two of the primary differences between good kids and teenagers with Christlike character are action and motivation. That's why we define *character* as *living out* Jesus' goodness every day by loving God and our neighbors.

Character is what extends faith beyond youth group. It's what we want our *good* youth group kids to take with them when they leave church so that wherever they go and whatever they do, they reflect and imitate Jesus. They're still generally good kids—but so much more.

Faith Beyond Youth Group

I (Jen) first met Ryan when he was a fourteen-year-old freshman at the church where I'd just started serving. Ryan was a tall, lanky teenager who was the quintessential *good* youth group kid. He went on to graduate as valedictorian of his high school class and become an Eagle Scout. His family was a pillar in our faith community, and Ryan was a regular at youth group gatherings. Regardless of what topic we were exploring, Ryan engaged—mostly by questioning everything I said.

Eventually, Ryan became part of our student leadership team, where he was instrumental in starting an end-of-the-year youth group banquet. At this banquet, student leaders affirmed each of their peers for their character—for the ways they lived out Jesus' goodness inside and outside youth group.

When he was seventeen, Ryan was a part of a mission trip to Rwanda, during which he visited a refugee camp. There, Ryan interacted with refugees from the Democratic Republic of Congo who had been in the camp for almost two decades. He heard (and saw) how they lacked healthcare and dental care. Before we left the camp, Ryan said he had found his life's purpose: he was going to become a dentist and return to the camp to care for refugees.

Now, a lot of young people utter a lot of well-intentioned words at the end of mission trips. But when Ryan says something, he follows through. He's now twenty-eight years old and a dentist with the US Navy.

When I recently saw Ryan, he recounted how difficult it was to serve in the military during COVID. Upon seeing how demoralized his colleagues were, he decided to do something about it. Ryan asked for a budget and set up a room on the ship where sailors could go to "find someone like them so they could belong." He led a book club. He started a series of fitness challenges. He created the equivalent of a Navy yearbook that affirmed his fellow sailors.

When he talked about his experience leading his colleagues through a global pandemic, he described how he relied on the Christlike character he had formed during youth group. Just as he had wanted his youth group friends to belong at the end-of-the-year banquet, he now wanted his fellow sailors to belong. He used the virtues of compassion, humility, and love—all of which were modeled and reinforced in our church—to tangibly care for those stationed on the ship with him.

Ryan has taken his faith with him to Japan, Australia, Spain, and many other places. As he makes decisions that allow him to practically love others across the globe, he consistently demonstrates his Christlike character.

And as for his dream?

Ryan hasn't made it back to that refugee camp.

Yet.

But he's pursuing a special classification within the Navy that will enable him to be part of the healthcare teams deployed by the military after global disasters. He is doing so because he still believes that compassionately loving others is his God-given purpose.

Like Ryan, the young people in your ministry want to see adults who authentically live out a faith that matters. They want to experiment with, figure out their relationship with, and feel out their commitment to a faith that can make a difference in who they are and how they relate to our world. Otherwise, they don't want it.

In short, they want a *faith beyond youth group*, which we unpack in the rest of this book and define as *Jesus-centered character that matters every day*. They want a faith that demonstrates not only that Christianity is true but also that Christianity is good.

We know you want that kind of faith for the young people you care about most. Every page of this book is geared to expand your missional imagination and equip you with practical ideas so that young people leave your ministry with faith beyond youth group.

We believe in you and know you can do it. We are with you and cheering for you.

And for young people.

REFLECTION QUESTIONS
---

1. Early on in this chapter, we asked, "What do we do in our ministries that truly forms the faith of students?" How would you answer this question?

2. Burnout is often the result of too little impact. When have you wondered if you're making too little impact? What compels you to stay in ministry even when you don't see a lot of impact?

3. We propose that "if teenagers' faith is just a youth group faith, it's too small to captivate their entire week . . . let alone their entire lives." How would a faith beyond youth group captivate young people's entire week and entire lives?

4. Our research team defines *character* as "living out Jesus' goodness every day by loving God and our neighbors." How does this definition compare to how you have previously thought about character? How would you contextualize it for your ministry?

5. To you, what is the difference between "good kids" and teenagers with Christlike character?

6. Why did you pick up this book? What are you hoping to gain through reading it? Think about the best ways

you tend to process content and form action steps. Is it marking up the book? Journaling alongside your reading? Processing with a colleague or your ministry team or with a leader from another church? Whatever works for you, put it in motion starting now!

BARE SPOTS AND BRIGHT SPOTS

Filling the Character Gaps

To me, character is a reminder that everyone is a little different! It is the thing that spreads us apart from people, but also the thing that pulls us closer to the right people! True character is hard to find these days because of all the fake narratives about who everyone has to be. Creating your own narrative and being your own main character in your story is important to living your life to the fullest.

High school student

Imagine you are scrolling your students' favorite social media platform when you come across one of your youth group kid's feeds. They're obviously at a wild party, surrounded by a group of friends who seem like they are having just a little too much fun. Everyone is lifting red Solo cups high for all the world to see.

What do you assume?

What do you wonder at that moment? What might you wonder about your students—and your own ministry effectiveness?

For one youth leader from a multiethnic church in our research, this was no hypothetical situation. In our interview with him, he admitted that at that moment, he wondered, "Did we make any impact at all? I hope I've taught you something other than that."

While we want to be careful about snap judgments and shaming kids for their choices, we can identify with this pain. And ultimately, this leader's hope is our hope. We bet it's your hope too. We want what we do *in* youth group to result in faith *beyond* youth group. We want our youth group kids to become young people whose character reflects Jesus and whose lives transform their world.

Sadly, all too often we see snapshots from students' lives that suggest gaps between the Christlike character we introduce at youth group and the way they live their daily lives. Teenagers might attend youth group Friday night but copy each other's math homework on Monday. They might serve at a food pantry with their friends on Saturday morning but lie to their parents about where they're going Saturday night. They might talk about Jesus' call to turn the other cheek at church on Sunday morning but act out road rage that very afternoon.

Research affirms these anecdotes. According to a study by the Josephson Institute Center for Youth Ethics, 50 percent of teenagers admit to cheating on tests, and 57 percent agree that "successful people do what they have to do to win, even if it involves cheating."[1] What's more, 80 percent confess to lying to their parents about "something important." And one-quarter of the teens in the survey believe it is acceptable to respond violently to other people when they're angry.[2] Despite teenagers' spotty moral choices and underdeveloped character commitments, 92 percent of kids "feel quite pleased with their ethical standards and conduct."[3]

A decade-long study by Notre Dame sociologist Christian Smith reinforces this conclusion. Smith writes:

> [Emerging adults] do not adequately know the moral landscape of the real world that they inhabit. And they do not adequately understand where they themselves stand in that real moral world. They need some better moral maps and better-equipped guides to show them the way around.[4]

Unfortunately, better-equipped guides can be hard to find given the prevalence of character gaps in parents, pastors, and other adults as well. As just one sensational example, in the 2019 college admissions scandal perhaps most notable for involving actress Lori Loughlin (many of us know her as Aunt Becky from *Full House*), family members bribed coaches and conspired to cheat on exams in order to ensure their children were admitted into prestigious colleges.[5]

Likewise, pastors also make the headlines when their character lapses. *Christianity Today*'s chronicling of Seattle megachurch pastor Mark Driscoll in the podcast series *The Rise and Fall of Mars Hill* showcases one among a slew of recent character stumbles in church leadership. Another is the firing of Carl Lentz from Hillsong East Coast for marital infidelity and abuse of power. Odds are good that you—and perhaps your students—can think of a leader you know who has struggled to live up to the way God wants them to love God and their neighbors.

Given these character gaps in adults, it's no wonder we see them in young people. As sociologist Christian Smith and practical theologian Kenda Creasy Dean both concluded from the extensive National Study of Youth and Religion, when it comes to kids' faith, "we get what we are."[6] Likewise, when it comes to character, we get what we are.

Three Reasons Character Gaps Exist

Why do such pronounced character gaps exist—not only in the general population but also in those who follow Jesus?

Based on our team's review of the literature as well as our ministry experience, we believe three factors prominently contribute to character gaps: our failure to understand God's character, the failure of the church to form character, and a shifting understanding of character.

1. Our Failure to Understand God's Character

Not surprisingly, three-quarters of US Christians view God as loving.[7] Perhaps more surprising is the way a *loving God* conjures up different images for different people. Researchers from Baylor University found that Americans picture God in four ways:

An authoritative God with power over our lives.

A benevolent God who answers our prayers and comforts us.

A critical God who judges us in the next life.

A distant God largely removed from day-to-day activities.[8]

Based on their analysis of the Baylor Religion Survey, as well as various national studies and interviews, these researchers concluded that how people view God is one of the "strongest predictors of a range of social and moral attitudes."[9] In other words, our character doesn't reflect only our Creator God; it reflects *who we create God to be*.

For example, after giving college students a psychological test in which he first asked them questions about themselves before asking them to imagine Jesus' personality, New Testament professor Scot McKnight concluded that "students are fashioning Jesus to be more like themselves."[10] When we fashion Jesus in our image, God's character starts to resemble ours rather than the other way around. This is a big deal because, as Father Gregory Boyle writes, "What matters, in the end, is what kind of God we believe in."[11]

2. The Failure of the Church to Form Character

Ask a church leader to tell you about their community, and you'll likely hear about size and doctrine, not character. A pastor might say, "We're a liturgical congregation that averages two hundred people on a Sunday morning." Likewise, a youth leader might tell you about the twenty young people who regularly attend their midweek gathering.

Many faith communities equate health with size and measure their success by attendance, not by how their community forms character. When I (Jen) shared about the importance of relational discipleship radically focused on Jesus with the elder board at the church where I serve as the volunteer youth pastor, an elder responded, "Teenagers won't show up for the God stuff, but they'll play laser tag."

This elder isn't alone in equating success with attendance. As theologian and philosopher James K. A. Smith writes, we've "confused keeping young people in the building with keeping them 'in Christ.'"[12] This confusion often causes churches to look at attendance numbers as the sole measure of success.

Sure, character counts. But churches have a hard time counting character.

In the fall of 2018, our Fuller Youth Institute research team found that the vast majority of the 386 nationwide youth leaders we surveyed did not include character and virtue development practices as part of their ministry goals and objectives.

Given our belief that character can be game-changing, our team has looked at this finding again and again. Even though it saddens us, we understand it.

Had the three of us (Kara, Jen, and Brad) taken this survey earlier in our youth ministry careers, we would have been among the vast majority of youth leaders who answered the question this way. While we care deeply about forming disciples with a faith beyond youth group, we likely wouldn't have included character formation on our list of ministry goals and objectives.

Instead, our ministry goals might have focused more on numbers and knowledge—how many young people we hoped to reach and the topics we planned to address in our youth ministry.

In hindsight, perhaps such a focus on knowledge is another reason the church is failing to form character. Many western Christians believe character is formed by "thinking correctly, believing truth, and making wise choices in light of the truth."[13] As a result, we prioritize teaching, often through one-way communication channels like sermons. (We'll explore why this is problematic in chapter 6 and offer tips on how to better teach for transformation.)

One youth leader from a suburban multiethnic church explained, "The primary function of youth ministries is information transfer. We have classes for specific grades or genders because we think we need to package information specifically so that people can understand. The issue I find with young people is that the longing of their hearts is not to *know* more but to *belong* more."

Or as we've heard from teenagers, showing up at youth group matters when they have "that internal feeling that I'm made to be here and I want to be here."

Sometimes teenagers experience that feeling most acutely in the wake of tragedy. When the mother of two teenagers in my (Jen's) youth ministry died after a horrific illness, they were both wrestling with the problem of evil, and what they needed most wasn't pat answers. It was our presence. When our youth group showed up at their mom's wake together and spent time looking at their photos and hearing them recount stories of their mom, they knew they belonged. Because they belonged, they showed up at youth group in the days, weeks, and months following their mom's death—even though they were angry with God.

Belonging matters deeply to this generation of young people. In fact, based on the Fuller Youth Institute's research over the past fifteen years, we are convinced that young people wrestle with three big questions:

Identity = *Who am I?*

Belonging = *Where do I fit?*

Purpose = *What difference can I make?*

For a deeper dive into identity, belonging, and purpose, please see *3 Big Questions That Change Every Teenager: Making the Most of Your Conversations and Connections* by Kara Powell and Brad M. Griffin.

While information helps shape our Jesus-centered answers to these questions, as that wise youth leader rightly perceived, today's teenagers long not for a greater amount of knowledge but rather for a greater sense of belonging. They crave unconditional relationships through which they can understand who they are in Christ and their place in God's story.

3. A Shifting Understanding of Character

Cultural shifts in America's understanding of character are a third factor contributing to the prevalence of character gaps. In *The Road to Character, New York Times* columnist David Brooks writes that "morality has been displaced by utility."[14]

This shift has changed how we talk about character. Nerdy researchers (like us!) have tracked the usage of character words in more than 5.2 million books published over the past decades. They found we "literally don't speak, write, or read about character as much these days."[15]

Given that we don't speak, write, or read about character like we used to, it's not surprising that character shifts can also be seen in what young people value. In one study, when tweens between the ages of eight and twelve were asked to rank a list of seven values (community feeling, image, benevolence, fame, self-acceptance, financial success, and achievement) in order of importance, 40 percent ranked fame as their top value.[16] In other words, they would rather be world-famous than well-formed.

Young people's obsession with fame coincides with the explosion of social media platforms that represent what Brooks classifies as a shift from a culture of humility to a culture of "Big Me," wherein people are encouraged "to see themselves as the center of the universe."[17]

Of course, the culture of "Big Me" is as prevalent in adults as it is in young people. One youth pastor from an affluent context bemoaned, "Our community is really big on perception. They are big on [being] image-based. They would rather look right than live right. Their identity is tied to their job, house, kids, and vacations. There are hidden issues within our context that do not ever really get to be addressed because looking right is prioritized over living right." This kind of mirage jeopardizes faith that lasts.

When we prioritize looking right over living right, teenagers inevitably learn "ethically challenged adult behaviors"—not just from those who are celebrities but from those they are closest to.[18] While examples of ethically challenged adult behavior permeate news headlines and social media hashtags, teenagers also see character gaps in the adults in their lives. They see us stretch the truth, ignore rules, and sidestep guidelines.

One of my (Brad's) most painful experiences in leading youth ministry happened because of the moral failure of a volunteer leader who, among other troubling behaviors, verbally harassed a group of students and smoked pot in front of them. While the students who knew what was happening felt pressure to keep quiet, a few brave young people finally broke the silence, and we quickly removed that leader from ministry.

What was remarkable about the students' processing afterward was their clarity about this leader's betrayal of them and of our church. "He was supposed to be the adult," as one student put it, but he proved to be untrustworthy. Once they gathered courage to speak up, they were clear that his actions did not match his position as a youth leader or his life as a Christ follower. Eventually, the gaps became more than they were willing to put up with.

Sometimes young people are the clearest about "living right." They aren't as morally ambiguous as we might assume.

This Generation We Love

At least in part because of these three reasons—our failure to understand God's character, the failure of the church to form character, and a shifting understanding of character—character gaps are prevalent across both news headlines and generations. For those of us who see those same character lapses and sometimes question if our ministry is developing a faith beyond youth group, it can be easy to assume the worst about young people. In fact, we know many adults who do.

Not us.

We are head-to-toe fans of young people. We believe teenagers are inherently good because they are created in the image of God who is good. We trust in *God's best* for all teenagers—including those connected to your youth ministry. We think you do too.

All the research and social media memes about the Millennial generation (those born from approximately 1980 to 2000, the youngest of whom is now a twentysomething) have cast a long shadow. So we're determined to shine a fresh spotlight on the uniqueness of Gen Z (those generally born from 2000 to 2015).[19]

We've done this by listening to young people. In fact, with every study our team has conducted over the years, *our conviction has grown that all good ministry—including and maybe especially ministry that yields consequential faith—starts by understanding the realities of today's young people.*

We've distilled what we've learned into an empathetic summary: Gen Z is anxious, adaptive, and diverse.[20]

Think of these three words—*anxious*, *adaptive*, and *diverse*—as your own SparkNotes or CliffsNotes study guide about teenagers. Part of what we love about today's young people is that in the midst of their anxiety, adaptivity, and diversity, they are finding new ways to creatively live out faith beyond youth group.

This Anxious Generation

Urgency about teenage anxiety, depression, and suicide has been growing the past decade and a half. Technology, the pace of teenagers' lives, parental pressures, and imbalances in brain chemistry often add up to too much stress.

Daniella is a senior who battles both anxiety and depression. Some days going to school is no problem; other days it's a battle for Daniella to make it through each class. As she describes, "I can't stop the messages in my mind that make me afraid I'm going to fail and want to avoid other people. I just want to stay in my bed and watch shows all day."

Her mom and dad have taken her to a professional therapist, who has helped some, but everyone (including Daniella) thinks a next good step is to see a psychiatrist to determine if prescription medicines would help. Daniella's story mirrors what many young people were experiencing even prior to the pandemic.

> » In 2019, 13 percent of adolescents reported having a major depressive episode—a 60 percent increase from 2007.[21]

> » For young people ages fifteen to twenty-four, American Indian or Alaskan Native youth had the highest rates of suicide, with White youth having the second highest.[22]

In our research and writing, we often call out the social location of those involved—meaning how each of us is shaped by our gender, race, ethnicity, social class, age, ability, religion, sexual orientation, and geography. Early in this book, we want to acknowledge our own social location. The three of us who are writing this are White. We're highly educated, middle to upper-middle class, straight, Protestant Christians.

We are diverse in some ways. Brad is male; Jen and Kara are female. We all grew up in different parts of the country (Kara in beach-loving Southern California, Brad in the rolling hills "horse country" of central Kentucky, and Jen in deep dish pizza–loving Illinois), in different types of families. Kara is the daughter of divorced parents. Jen is a first-generation college student in her family. Brad is a farm-kid-turned-city-dweller. In the midst of our similarities and our differences, we cannot deny that our social location shapes everything about us, including our understanding of character and the ways we lead and love others.

» While the overall suicide rate among White teenagers is higher than among Black young people, that gap was closing pre-pandemic. Suicide attempts by Black adolescents rose 73 percent from 1991 to 2017, compared with 18 percent among White teenagers.[23]

» For all age groups, the suicide rate for Asian or Pacific Islander individuals increased 16 percent between 2014 and 2019.[24]

These underlying conditions intensified during the COVID-19 pandemic—and beyond it.

» Across generations, anxiety tripled in the US during the first year of the pandemic (from 8.1 percent to 25.5 percent), and depression almost quadrupled (from 6.5 percent to 24.3 percent).[25]

» In multiple studies, people of color (especially Latinos) reported greater stress and mental health symptoms. White teens were more likely to report having adequate access to mental health resources—at a still-paltry

32 percent—compared with only 19 percent of Black teens and 21 percent of Hispanic young people.[26]

» Suicide rates among Black young people ages 10–24 years increased 36.6 percent between 2018 and 2021, the largest increase of any racial group.[27] In 2021, Black students were more likely than Asian, Hispanic, and White students to attempt suicide.[28]

» A recent study of teenagers in the UK found that by age eleven, girls were 30 percent more likely than boys to suffer from poor mental health. By the time girls turn eighteen, they are twice as likely as boys to struggle.[29]

» According to a striking 2023 CDC report, teen girls in the US reported record levels of sadness and suicidal ideation in fall 2021. Almost 60 percent of female students experienced persistent feelings of sadness or hopelessness over the course of the year, and nearly 25 percent made a suicide plan. Likewise, close to 70 percent of LGBQ+ students reported experiencing persistent feelings of sadness or hopelessness, and almost 25 percent reported having attempted suicide during the previous year.[30]

The same CDC report summarizes, "Across almost all measures of substance use, experiences of violence, mental health, and suicidal thoughts and behaviors, female students are faring more poorly than male students. These differences, and the rates at which female students are reporting such negative experiences, are stark."[31] Anecdotally, I (Kara) don't know a single US family with teenage girls who is not navigating mental health concerns.

Helping Anxious Young People Move Their Faith Beyond Youth Group

We want churches and families—including your church and the families in your community—to be the *first places* teenagers go with their stress and anxiety. We want teenagers to think, *I can talk about this at church.*

Recent research shows that being part of a faith community tends to be positive for young people's mental well-being. While one-third of young people say they are not flourishing in their mental and emotional health, the more religious or spiritual a young person is, the more likely they are to say they are "flourishing a lot." What's more, young people who are currently connected to a faith community report greater flourishing in their mental and emotional health.[32]

For more in-depth tools to help you navigate your students' mental health challenges and nurture a mental health–friendly youth ministry, visit Fuller YouthInstitute.org/AnxiousWorld.

The students at St. Luke's United Methodist Church in Indianapolis know they can talk about mental health at church and that their church wants them to flourish. Like most youth leaders, Travis Bannon, the church's associate director of youth ministry, was increasingly encountering students who were struggling with mental health, including one eleventh grader who pronounced, "Right now, you either have mental health struggles or you're caring for friends who do."

Travis and his team felt called to offer training *for* teens, unlike much of mental health training that's *about* teens.[33] After seeking input from the mental health professionals in the congregation, Travis scheduled a Saturday morning training titled "Teen Responders." The stated goal of Teen Responders was to equip teenagers to help their friends, but Travis and the counselors involved knew that attendees would also gain help for their own stress and anxiety.

The two hundred spots (one hundred for teenagers and one hundred for adults) quickly filled. Only fifteen of the students were from Travis' church; the rest were from local schools, which had heard about Teen Responders and had decided to promote the training to all their students. Travis knew they had struck a nerve when his youth group kids started getting all-class emails from multiple teachers encouraging attendance at the training.

All of the training content was provided by mental health professionals who donated their time to cover topics such as "Boundaries and Self-Care," "Healthy Coping Strategies," and "Recognizing and Responding to Crisis." Throughout the morning, volunteer therapists were available on-site to meet with teenagers who felt overwhelmed or triggered.

One highlight was when students moved around the church meeting hall, visiting different tables and gathering items for their own "mental health first aid kits" (in small cardboard boxes). Teenagers loved collecting the mostly donated tools, such as fidgets and stress balls, sleep masks, emotion wheels, and lists of online and phone resources.

At the end of the day, students received special Teen Responder pins and stickers. Travis hopes that Teen Responders will become so well-known in their community that hurting students who see these pins and stickers will know those peers are safe places to share their pain. Simultaneously, Teen Responders will demonstrate their character by tangibly loving those struggling with anxiety and stress.

On the heels of that successful Saturday training, Travis and his church were invited by a local high school to distribute mental health resources, as well as invited by the Department of Corrections to repeat their training at multiple local juvenile detention centers.

Interested in finding out how your church might be able to host the same sort of mental health training for your community? See TeenResponders .com for more information.

As one student gushed after the Saturday training, "I didn't realize how much I was shouldering my friends' burdens. And how much I needed practical help like this."

This Adaptive Generation

Part of why Teen Responders is so effective is that it taps into a second attribute of young people: adaptability. Also referred to as resilience, perseverance, or grit, *adaptability* is a young person's ability to accomplish particular goals or tasks in the face of challenges and ambiguity. As you've probably seen in your own youth ministry, a young person's adaptability is "the difference between treading water and swimming."[34]

As the oldest of four girls, fifteen-year-old Sylvia embodied many typical firstborn traits—she was responsible, hardworking, and consistently prioritized what was best for her three younger sisters. All that was put to the test when the girls' mom fell sick with an aggressive cancer and passed away, leaving the four girls with no choice but to move in with their dad, who had been emotionally distant the girls' entire lives.

Given the absence of support and guidance from her dad, Sylvia could have shifted into survival mode and prioritized what was best for her. Or, on the other extreme, she could have placed her sisters' needs ahead of her own to the point that she lost herself. While only a high school sophomore, she adapted and found the right middle ground, in which she focused more on her own studies and extracurricular activities during the week and more on her sisters during the weekend. It was a full—and sometimes exhausting—last few years of high school, but Sylvia graduated with both a full scholarship to a prestigious school and the relationships she desired with her sisters.

Adaptability by the Numbers

Just like Sylvia, many Gen Zers are remarkably creative and tough. They have learned to navigate ever-changing technology, financial challenges, family conflict, academic pressures, friendship drama, and racial prejudice—often with impressive wisdom and dignity.

» The average sixteen- to seventeen-year-old views themselves as "often" resilient. In a longitudinal study, Australian adolescents scored themselves as 26.5 out of 40 on a resilience scale. Boys ranked themselves with higher scores (27.6) than girls (25.5).[35]

» What researchers call a "growth mindset," or the perspective that "my ability and competence grow with my effort, strategies, and help from others," has been described as perhaps the single most important factor in perseverance in academic pursuits.[36]

» Teenagers with close relationships with one or both of their parents during early and mid-adolescence show higher levels of resilience at ages sixteen to seventeen (by almost 3 points on a scale of 1–40).[37]

With the advent of the smartphone in 2007—right around the time today's teenagers were born—and the increase of accessibility to data and Wi-Fi nearly everywhere and all the time—this generation has grown up in an era of rapid technological adaptation like no previous generation in world history. We've been trying to catch up and keep up as adults, but for young people, the digital world is the only world they've ever known.

The COVID-19 pandemic added a new layer of needed adaptivity—from quarantines to at-home learning to lots (and lots) of changed plans. All that change adds up. *For the next decade, every student in your ministry will be a pandemic-impacted kid.*

While they're undoubtedly more adaptive than ever, many of them also missed key social and emotional development steps along the way. A whole cohort of kids entered the pandemic as children and emerged from it as adolescents. They may be skipping notes we take for granted in the music of relationships because they never learned how to sight-read or how to follow the cues.

As one leader told us in fall 2022, "Freshmen are acting like seventh graders." To say it another way, it's hard to tell how the kids who missed kindergarten in 2020 will still be affected when they hit your high school group in 2029.

The Role of Struggle in Adaptivity

One of the themes of the research on young people—and the rest of this book—is that young people's pain can build perseverance. Some of our most adaptive teenage heroes are those who face tough constraints that birth new creativity.

Such as the 9.4 percent of young people diagnosed with attention-deficit/hyperactivity disorder (ADHD),[38] who have to work extra hard in school to make sense of their classes and homework.

And the more than one in three US teenagers who have grown up in poverty or low-income households[39] and have had to figure out how to access resources that the other half of teens often take for granted.

Or children of immigrant families who certainly navigate a host of struggles but also have unique strengths related to family cohesion, passion in pursuing goals, and greater cognitive development given their fluent bilingualism.[40] As an example, Asian American teenagers who hold in tension at least two different cultures and experience marginalization often develop overlooked strengths such as versatility and cultural competencies.[41]

As will become clear, we believe all generations—including teenagers—should work and advocate for justice and flourishing for all people. We want this because God wants it. We believe the creativity born from teenagers' adaptivity, paired with our intentional support, can help us get closer to God's vision for all of us.

Tapping into Adaptability Beyond Youth Group

Inspired by the vitality of the young people in her church, Nancy English-Fletcher realized that the ethnically diverse teenagers at Grace First Presbyterian Church were adaptable and wanted to serve the community beyond their annual mission trip. As a new youth pastor in the Los Angeles area, Nancy was convicted that she needed to shift from doing youth ministry "to and for" very capable teenagers to ministry "with and by" them.

So Nancy began handing over the keys of leadership to her students. She told them she wanted and needed them to plan youth group meetings, service activities, and fun events. She would be engaged and supportive, but they needed to be in the driver's seat. From Sunday morning youth group to a new community food drive to art and cooking classes, everything became led by young people.

Eventually, the teenagers felt so engaged that when the church had its next business meeting, not only did students attend but they came with amendments they wanted to suggest! Thanks to

Nancy's responsive leadership, this creative group of young disciples went from being spectators in the stands to being players running plays on the field by tangibly leading and loving others.[42]

This Diverse Generation

Arguably, young people today are the most diverse generation in US history. Teenagers are proud of that diversity. For this generation, valuing diversity isn't just an expectation; it's nonnegotiable.

Diversity by the Numbers

» While about two-thirds of all US residents are White today, that percentage drops to half for those under eighteen. That's right—50 percent of US young people are White, and 50 percent are people of color. (If you're curious, those under eighteen comprise just over 22 percent of the total US population.)[43]

» Currently, about 98 percent of Americans live in a county with a growing Latina/o population, and 95 percent live in a county where the Asian population is on the rise. Overall, ethnic diversity is rising in nineteen out of every twenty US counties.[44]

» According to a recent Gallup study, the percentage of adults who identify as lesbian, gay, bisexual, transgender, or something other than cisgender and heterosexual is now 7.1 percent, double what it was in 2012. For the oldest Gen Zers, that percentage is roughly 21 percent—or one in five.[45]

» Approximately 14 percent of national public school students are categorized as "disabled" (which is 11 percent higher than in 2001). The most common category is learning disabilities, followed by speech or language impairments, other health impairments, autism, and developmental delays.[46]

» Today's teenagers also approach their personal faith with more openness to the integration of diverse viewpoints. More than half (55 percent) report they don't feel a need to be connected to a specific religion, and 47 percent feel they could fit in with many religions or faith traditions.[47]

We recognize that questions about LGBTQ+ identity are both prominent and controversial within many churches and traditions. Our purpose in including language about sexuality and LGBTQ+ teenagers in this book is not to take a particular theological position on human sexuality but rather to urge you as a caring adult and community to listen and empathize and to uphold the dignity of every person made in the image of God.

Diversity Beyond Youth Group

As one member of Gen Z posted online, "Our schools are diverse, our workplaces are diverse, and our friend groups are diverse. If your church isn't at least as diverse as the school we grew up in, we will question you as an organization."[48]

Motivated by the way her church, Southside Methodist, was elevating the voices and contributions of neurodiverse adults in their Jacksonville, Florida, community, youth pastor Amy Franks felt led to do the same with young people.[49] Realizing the importance of partnering with other leaders who had more expertise serving teenagers with a range of abilities, Amy contacted the leader of the local Young Life Capernaum Project, a national ministry that creates spaces of belonging for teens and young adults with intellectual and developmental disabilities. Working together, the church and Young Life started a new Capernaum Club. Every week, about twelve neurodiverse young people ages fourteen to twenty-two would gather along with ten to twenty neurotypical teenagers from Amy's youth group who were volunteer "buddies."

One of the many blessings of this partnership has been how Southside Methodist as a whole, and the youth ministry in particular, has been quick to serve. There has been no shortage of teenage helpers from Amy's youth ministry, with some teenagers (especially those who feel like they don't fit in as well at youth group) preferring Capernaum Club to youth group. Not only that, but her church kids often find it easier to invite unchurched friends to serve with them at Capernaum Club than to attend Southside's youth group. Amy has also been inspired by how her youth group students spend time with their neurodiverse buddies outside the club, accompanying them to baseball games or having meals together.

Eager to find a next step to continue building relationships with diverse young people who were in their mid- and late twenties, Amy secured support from her church to start Happy Brew Coffee Shop. The goals of Happy Brew are to create a space in which neurotypical and neurodiverse teenagers and young adults can work alongside each other, and individuals and families of all abilities can enjoy a meaningful cup of coffee.

To find out more about the "poss-abilities" championed by Happy Brew, visit HappyBrew.org.

You may also find it helpful to check out Princeton Seminary Institute of Youth Ministry's (IYM) resources and training titled "Cultivating God's Brainforest," created in partnership with FYI through a subgrant as part of this overall project on character-forming discipleship. Alongside neurodivergent young people, parents, and youth workers, IYM developed this training to help leaders better understand and engage the gifts of neurodiversity within Christian congregations. Learn more at TheologyAndNeurodiversity.com/Resources.

Happy Brew has been physically designed to accommodate a wide array of disabilities—offering everything from braille menus to sensory phone stations for those with autism to adult changing tables in the bathrooms. Open Wednesday through Sunday and operated by a team of young staff who are 60 percent neurodiverse and 40 percent neurotypical, Happy Brew employs a full-time occupational therapist who coordinates an internship program to connect diverse young people's skills with the coffee shop's needs. While Amy and her team raised an impressive amount of money for start-up expenses, since they use a church building and can keep other costs relatively low, Amy is optimistic that revenue from coffee sales will largely cover their ongoing expenses.

According to Amy, a highlight of Happy Brew has been all they learn from neurodiverse young people. One day at Capernaum Camp, Tommy decided he was done walking. He sat down on the ground and asked Amy and another adult nearby to "carry me." As Amy later summarized, "Tommy's message was the message we needed at Happy Brew. Our regular prayer—inspired by Tommy—is that we would know it is God who is carrying us."

A Portrait of Faith Beyond Youth Group

Imagine you are scrolling your students' favorite social media platform again, and you come across one of your youth group kid's feeds. Instead of prompting you to question, "Did youth group make any impact at all?," what if their feed was evidence of faith beyond youth group?

What if, instead of seeing partying teenagers lifting red Solo cups high, you saw:

Teenagers leading both inside and outside the church building because you've taught them the basics of following Jesus, which now shape and define their lives.

Young people marching in peaceful protests because their Christlike character compels them to stand up to injustice.

College students showing hospitality at their dorms and workplaces because they are committed to loving their neighbors as themselves.

Forming Character and Faith Beyond Youth Group in Any Ministry

The three examples we just shared are from real-life stories of how youth leaders like you have seen young people from their ministries exhibit faith-filled character.

What's extraordinary about these examples is how very *ordinary* they are. You don't have to work at a certain type of ministry to focus on character formation. Character formation works in any denomination, in any size ministry, and with any size budget. Character formation doesn't require fancy programs or slick youth rooms. Instead, it harnesses the power of relationships to cultivate trust, model faith, teach for transformation, practice together, and make meaning.

You can do this.

We know you can, because in the research we describe in the next chapter, we encountered dozens of leaders like you who formed character in young people that enabled them to live a faith beyond youth group—both before and after graduation.

REFLECTION QUESTIONS

1. What are some examples of recent character gaps you have seen—in yourself? Young people? Celebrities? How about in the church?

2. Researchers have concluded that how people view God is one of the "strongest predictors of a range of social and moral attitudes."[50] How do you view God? How do those connected to your ministry view God? How do you see those views of God reflected in character?

3. What evidence have you seen of the culture of "Big Me"? How does the culture of "Big Me" make it harder to form character in young people?

4. What signs of anxiety do you see in the teenagers you know? How is the national mental health crisis showing up in your particular ministry?

5. How have you observed young people being adaptable and accomplishing particular goals or tasks even in the face of small and large obstacles?

6. What types of diversity are most evident in the young people in your life? How might that diversity affect how they live out their faith beyond youth group?

THREE

A NEW COMPASS

Finding Faith Beyond Youth Group

When one high school girl went home after each Sunday's youth night at her Catholic parish, she eagerly told her family that she felt God speaking to her through the prayers and discussions. Based on the change he saw in his daughter, her dad decided to return to mass. Her youth leader reflected, "God transformed her heart, not just for herself, but now she's bringing so many other people to God with such a humble, joyful spirit." For this girl, what happened at youth group did not stay at youth group. It transformed her life and her family.

For a handful of students from a different church, when a friend of a friend made a joke about George Floyd's 2020 murder, rather than just let it go, they felt it was so wrong that they spoke up. Later, they started a group on social media to proclaim, "These things are inappropriate. As a generation we need to put a stop to this." For this small group, what happened at youth group did not stay at youth group. Instead, convictions formed in their ministry empowered teenagers to live out their faith all week long.

When a teenager felt God calling her to focus on justice issues but her family did not support her, she started regularly texting questions to her youth pastor. Those conversations equipped her to speak up for herself and respectfully tell her parents why justice ministry was important to her. What happened at youth group did not stay at youth group. Instead, her youth ministry gave her the courage to use her voice in new ways outside of youth group.

In each of these stories, a young person lived out Jesus' goodness every day by loving God and their neighbors. That's *character*. In each of these stories, a teenager demonstrated Jesus-centered character that matters every day. That's *faith beyond youth group*.

Our Research Journey

These three stories all emerged from our Faith Beyond Youth Group research, in which our Fuller Youth Institute team set out to explore how character formation could fuel discipleship and help answer real questions that make a difference in forming lasting faith in young people.[1]

The Fuller Youth Institute has been studying lasting faith, or what we call Sticky Faith, since 2005. While Sticky Faith focuses primarily on developing a faith that lasts into adulthood, Faith Beyond Youth Group explores character as the vehicle for both faith longevity *and* faith vibrancy throughout each week. To find out more about our numerous related resources and how they can equip you and the families in your church to build a faith that lasts, visit FullerYouthInstitute.org/StickyFaith.

First, our research team surveyed 378 youth leaders like you to unearth their ministry goals and evaluate whether these included character formation. We also paid attention to their initial response to words like *character* and *virtue*.[2]

We paired these youth leader interactions with a broad, cross-disciplinary analysis of over two hundred academic and popular sources about character formation, some of which we've already introduced you to and many of which we'll draw from later in this book.

Next, our team conducted ninety-six phone interviews with youth ministry leaders from churches and parachurch organizations across the country. In choosing leaders to interview for ninety minutes, we tried to be as inclusive as possible, inviting leaders from across the spectrum of church size, denomination, and ethnocultural background. We were especially pleased that our interviewees were 27 percent Hispanic/Latina/o, 22 percent White, 19 percent Asian/Asian American, 19 percent Black/African American, and 13 percent Other/Multiracial.

After that, we transcribed and analyzed the interviews.[3] Along the way, we regularly sought advice and feedback from a diverse team of scholars and practitioners. Their fingerprints are (thankfully) found throughout our work and make it so much better.

Finally, we completed seven site visits to noteworthy faith communities, each of which was distinct from the others in some way (such as ethnicity, size, theological tradition, and/or location). During our team's site visits, we observed worship and youth group gatherings in order to see character formation happening in real-world settings. We also interviewed senior pastors, youth pastors, youth ministry volunteers, parents, and teenagers themselves in order to further explore their character and faith journeys.

One of the many reasons *character* is a loaded term is the way in which some of us associate it with specific behaviors, like sexual morality or the fight against a multitude of injustices.

Based on our review of the research literature, Scripture, and the hundreds of conversations our team has had with youth leaders, we have intentionally tried not to reduce character to or conflate it with one specific behavior.

Character is never *one* behavior, nor is it ever merely the absence of certain behaviors. Character should never be used to shame anyone. In contrast, the depiction of character throughout Scripture is filled with grace.

Character is holistic. It is both who we are (our identity) and what we do (how we live out our faith and our love for God and our neighbors).

Character is never about behaviorism—or an attempt to earn God's love or our place of belonging in a specific community. Instead, living out Christlike character is our response to being wholly and completely loved by God.

As you read this book and apply our team's findings to your unique context, we encourage you to consider whatever character traits might be most important to your community. Generously consider virtues that you may have previously neglected. As you do, remember that character is never just one behavior. It is the holistic living out of Jesus' goodness every day by loving God and our neighbors.

How Character Formation Has Harmed Marginalized People

While we're tremendously excited about our research on character-forming discipleship, we also want to acknowledge the ways in which efforts to develop character have historically harmed marginalized people.

In some instances, character development has been used to promote compliance with a dominant culture's way of life—especially White normative culture in the US. Teachers often feel this acutely as they teach character. According to one teacher from Washington, DC, "When kids misbehave, we urge them to show more character; students who do well win character awards at special assemblies; we start giving points for integrity, and then integrity starts to mean following directions, and then we start taking integrity points away. . . . Character starts to look a little more like compliance."[4]

People of color have also been harmed by character formation when dominant cultures intentionally or unintentionally idolize "good character" rather than work to fix the systemic issue that necessitated the virtue in the first place. One youth pastor from a Latina/o congregation shared, "I don't want to idolize perseverance when the reality is that perseverance could be avoided if we changed certain systems that make you struggle and persevere. We could do something about poverty and then those who are poor would not have to persevere."

Similarly, in his book *Doing Christian Ethics from the Margins*, Miguel De La Torre shares how, during his childhood, his mother decided to lie about her employment experience in order to get a job to feed her family. While ethicists from the dominant class might wax eloquently about the virtue of honesty in relation to his mother's actions, De La Torre notes how her actions were in service of meeting the basic needs of her family while retaining her dignity, despite society's efforts to marginalize them. In situations like these, it's important to be mindful of how racial identity, ethnic background, immigration status, and socioeconomic class interact with ethical decisions. As De La Torre warns, "Virtues, no matter how desirable, can be imposed to ensure the subservience of the marginalized."[5] True character is complex.

As with so many other areas of scholarship, another problematic aspect of character development work is that it has been historically dominated by White voices. Among other complications, narrow perspectives impact how we interpret character in Scripture. Too often, people of color are harmed by character formation efforts when the culturally dominant community insists that its interpretations of the Bible are more "objective" and "true," sometimes excluding or deprioritizing other perspectives.[6]

Our team grieves character development practices that have harmed people of color and other marginalized groups. *Character formation should never be used as a tool to oppress or enact violence upon others.* Period.

We also acknowledge the limitations of our own research. Despite good-faith efforts to track down diverse sources, our literature review includes a disproportionate number of White authors. Fewer people of color participated in our research, particularly in the initial survey, than we would have liked.[7] We had very little Indigenous representation in this project. While diverse advisers spoke into our work at every step, no one culture is a monolith, and there are multiple perspectives we have missed.

We acknowledge and apologize for the limitations of our work and want you to know that throughout it, we have tried to take into account the current and historical critiques of character development work rightfully raised by people of color. We are grateful for our diverse and thoughtful team of FYI colleagues and researchers who help us attend to the intersections of culture, ethnicity, gender, and other dynamics of social location. With their help, we've taken steps to make our research more inclusive of diverse people and perspectives and have implemented best practices for researching diverse populations throughout this project. For where we have missed the mark, we apologize and ask for grace, and we hope to keep learning.

The Faith Beyond Youth Group Compass

Given the prevalence of character gaps in the United States, equipping young people with the Christlike character they need to live out their faith beyond youth group might seem impossible.

It's not.

Our research has yielded a five-point compass that will guide you in forming the character of young people in your own context. While the rest of this book unpacks this compass, we want you to have some initial framing about these five points ahead of time.

We've intentionally chosen to depict our findings from the Faith Beyond Youth Group research as a *compass*, not as a checklist or linear process, because it is a navigational tool, a way to orient ourselves in a particular direction using a map in order to reach a particular destination. When we turn, the compass shifts and we explore different terrain. While the order of the compass points listed in this book reflects the most common chronological order we saw in churches, it is by no means the only order.

The five points of the Faith Beyond Youth Group Compass are cultivate trust, model growth, teach for transformation, practice together, and make meaning.

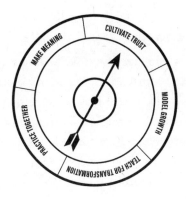

Cultivate Trust

According to our interviews, youth ministries like yours are already highly relational. This finding was so salient in our research that the first point of our Faith Beyond Youth Group Compass, *cultivate trust*, asks how youth ministries can best leverage the relational strengths they already possess to develop character-forming identity, belonging, and purpose. Our relationships as leaders can build faith beyond youth group when they are permeated with trust and punctuated with empathy and authenticity.

Model Growth

Modeling is showing others who we are every day. Teenagers wonder, *Are you for real? Are you the same outside church as you are inside?* They're watching for what our everyday actions reveal. Do we *model growth*? When we live consistently, we let them know they can trust us with the parts of themselves they might be hesitant to bring to church—including their doubts, questions, mistakes, and hurts. As youth leaders, we can model consistency and integrity as we live everyday faith imperfectly, both within and beyond the church—so teenagers can follow us as we follow Christ (1 Cor. 11:1).

Teach for Transformation

Youth leaders value teaching. We believe it is imperative to faith and character formation. Yet so often our teaching has been focused on one-way information transmission, which seldom forms actual character. Throughout our Faith Beyond Youth Group research, we were amazed at the innovative ways youth leaders like you formed character by *teaching for transformation*—building on the work of others, telling stories, asking questions, and commissioning others with authority, which are all strategies Jesus used with his followers to form their character. When character is taught in a way that transforms young people's identities, they leave with faith beyond youth group.

Practice Together

Everyday life is the training ground for character formation. Young people are sent out to test the virtues they've learned in relationships through modeling and teaching in the church and youth ministry. For example, they've "caught" and been "taught" the virtue of forgiveness in community, and now they get to apply that wisdom to everyday life within their families, relationships, schools, and communities. As we *practice together*, we walk with young people through a cycle of action and reflection, helping them try on service, leadership, hospitality, and holistic practices that move faith out of their heads and into their hands and feet. Through the struggles and victories of everyday life, young people develop character competence and, eventually, begin to own their faith.

Make Meaning

When we create environments where teenagers can reflect on what happens in their lives, we help them understand who they are and who they can be in Jesus. In the midst of once-a-year and week-to-week experiences, teenagers wonder, *What happened? What does it mean? Where is God? What now?* Faithful leaders guide students through these cycles of action and reflection; we *make meaning*, tapping into the power of naming experiences, evaluating our actions, and connecting to the larger biblical narrative before we go out and try again.

Who am I?. . . To know who you are is to be oriented in moral space, a space in which questions arise about what is good and bad, what is worth doing and what not, what has meaning and importance to you . . . there are two ways that we can fail to have [moral orientation]. I can be ignorant of the lie of the land around me—not knowing the important locations which make it up or how they relate to each other. This ignorance can be cured by a good map. But then I can be lost in another way if I don't know how to place myself on this map. —Charles Taylor[8]

The topography of character-forming discipleship is as diverse and layered as today's young people. When it comes to character formation, there is no one-size-fits-all solution or easy equation for it—no matter how much we might like there to be one. That's why you won't see a formula for character in this book.

X + Y does not always = Christlike character.

Instead, our team's prayer is that the Faith Beyond Youth Group Compass will point you in the right direction to form character in your teenagers while also giving you the room to contextualize the five points for your specific ministry setting. To help you do this, we'll share lots of diverse stories and ideas from our research and our own ministry experiences. We hope they will spark your creativity and inspire you to leverage the game-changing work of character formation in your ministry. As you do, teenagers will leave your ministry with the gift of faith that extends well beyond youth group.

REFLECTION QUESTIONS

1. Think about the three examples from our research that began this chapter. What examples from your own ministry would you add to this list of how you have seen character enable young people to live out their faith beyond youth group?

2. Our research focused on seven key virtues: faith, hope, love, forgiveness, compassion, perseverance, and humility. What are some other virtues you would add to this list? How are they particularly important to your faith community?

3. "Character formation should never be used as a tool to oppress or enact violence upon others." How have you seen or experienced character formation used as an oppressive tool? In what ways have you (perhaps inadvertently) contributed to this?

4. Review the five points on the Faith Beyond Youth Group Compass. Which are you particularly interested in learning more about and exploring in your ministry? Why?

FOUR

CULTIVATE TRUST

How Empathy and Authenticity Set the Speed of Trust

> There is one thing that is common to every individual, relationship, team, family, organization, nation, economy, and civilization throughout the world—one thing which, if removed, will destroy the most powerful government, the most successful business, the most thriving economy, the most influential leadership, the greatest friendship, the strongest character, the deepest love.... That one thing is trust.
>
> Stephen M. R. Covey[1]

A 2:04 a.m. phone call from a youth group kid is never good news.

That was Oscar's first thought when he saw that Marcus—an eleventh grader from his small group—was calling.

Sure enough, Marcus was calling to confess that he had just slept with Olivia, another eleventh grader from their church. He and Olivia had previously talked about their mutual commitment to stopping their physical relationship short of sex, but in the heat of the moment, that intention had fallen by the wayside. Not only did Marcus feel guilty about having sex but he was also disappointed he hadn't been able to follow through on his and Olivia's commitment to each other.

Oscar was honored that Marcus felt safe telling him what happened and arranged to meet the young man for breakfast later that morning. He then spent the next thirty minutes doing what you or I (Kara) would have done in the same situation. He searched for relevant Scripture passages, jotted down key thoughts and questions, and prayed that God would give him wisdom.

Seven hours later, after ordering bacon and eggs at their favorite diner, Oscar shared with Marcus that faith is a journey that includes our sexuality but is ultimately about so much more. No matter our mistakes, God is so good that, according to Romans 2:4, it is God's kindness that leads us to repentance.

Eager to hear what might be sinking in, Oscar paused and asked, "So, Marcus, what do you think about what I've been saying?"

Marcus silently stared at the Formica table for a few seconds before giving Oscar full eye contact. "Oscar, what you're saying makes sense. But actually, I didn't sleep with Olivia last night." He continued, "I just wanted to *see how you would respond to me if I had*."

Oscar gulped.

As did I (Kara) when Oscar told me this story a few weeks later.

Our youth ministries are full of anxious, adaptive, and diverse kids like Marcus who wonder if they can trust us with their biggest secrets and failures.

Your students are likely more subtle than to pull stunts like this one. They are constantly assessing whether they can trust you to be there for them when—not *if*, but *when*—they make a mistake or their life unravels.

It may be what motivates that eighth grader to push boundaries or outright break youth group rules. Or what prompts that sophomore to share a painful interaction with his stepdad and then watch to see if you lean into his pain or side with "the adult." Or what spurs a few seniors to criticize your leadership—loudly enough that you and a few other kids hear—and then wait to see if you'll be defensive.

Given our research on faith and character, we are convinced that if students like Marcus don't trust their youth leaders, they aren't likely to have a faith *within* youth group. Let alone *beyond* youth group.

We Can Cultivate Character at the "Speed of Trust"

We're grateful for the youth leaders who dove into relational discipleship with teenagers during the pandemic—even when they couldn't gather with students in the same room. Every week, we heard stories of creative adults who sat six feet away from youth group kids in front yards, back yards, and church parking lots—making sure they stayed in touch with how their students were *really* doing. Leaders who dropped off care packages at young people's doorsteps or used food delivery services to surprise students with meals.

We just wish that such innovative relationship building was more common. COVID-19 revealed how hard it is for leaders to expand faith outside of programming. In some of the most disturbing ministry data released during the pandemic, just 10 percent of 2,500 thirteen- to twenty-five-year-olds surveyed by Springtide Research Institute had a pastor or church staff member reach out to them during the first year of the pandemic.[2] You read that right: only 1 out of 10 received contact from a faith leader.

But here's some more inspiring data: *the same study by Springtide revealed that nearly 70 percent of those young people say they won't take relationships for granted anymore.*[3]

A new door is available to build transformative relationships with young people. Based on our research, we believe *trust is the key that unlocks that door.*

The Trust-Building Soil of Consistency and Closeness

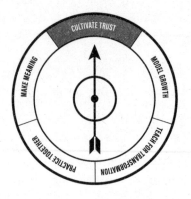

We can cultivate character and faith beyond youth group at "the speed of trust,"[4] which is why our first compass point is *cultivate trust.* We define trust as *teenagers' confidence that when they offer something personally important to a leader, that leader will act in their best interests.*

Trust is the underpinning in our five-point Faith Beyond Youth Group Compass. In the long race of cultivating character, it is like our pace car. As we log lap after lap of relationship with students, we can never go faster in building faith and character than the speed of students' trust in us.

Often the pace of trust is slower than we desire or expect. Teenagers may have been disappointed in the past when they have courageously shared what's meaningful to them with adults—their thoughts, feelings, stories, insecurities, dreams, and relationships. No wonder teenagers are understandably sheepish—or downright refuse—to trust us now.

What does it take for us to regain young people's confidence that we will treat their gifts—and them—with dignity? Both our research and parallel education studies point to two key precursors to cultivating trust: consistency and closeness.[5]

Consistency = our relational longevity.
Closeness = our relational proximity.

Consistency and closeness are the essential soil in which trust can grow.

As we observed in research site visits, no part of this trust-building cultivation can be sped up or skipped. Danny, the youth pastor at a multigenerational Chinese American church, described a middle schooler, Min, who decided to follow Jesus at camp soon after she started attending their church. Inspired by her new faith, Min initially loved serving at the church and joined the student leadership team. But as she transitioned to high school, she asked Danny, "Why doesn't our church do more events that I would like more?"

Min raised this question with Danny repeatedly. Each time, Danny listened and tried to help her understand that the church needed people who understood the church wasn't just about them.

"My small group leader is someone I trust with the deepest parts of my life . . . things I've told no one else."

At camp during Min's senior year, the speaker elevated the same message about putting others first that Danny had been sharing with Min for three years. On the last night of the camp, in large part because of her closeness with Danny and the consistency of his influence, Min stood before all of the teenagers and shared, "You know what, I've learned that here in my faith community, it's *not just about me.*"

Sure, it would have been nice for it to have sunk in more quickly for Min. And we've all had students who don't grasp something we've been repeating for years—and then someone else says it *once* and it clicks. But odds are good that Danny's consistency and closeness—and our own—loosen the soil of students' hearts so that those seeds of truth can take root and bear fruit.

Trust as a Portal to Character-Forming Community

On the surface, it appears that it was Min's long-term, up-close relationship with Danny that helped her grow in characteristics like perseverance and selflessness. As we will see in chapter 5 on modeling growth, God certainly cultivated faith beyond youth group in Min through Danny's vital example as a trusted mentor. But one of Danny's most important functions was to connect Min with the broader community.

Through Danny as one of her initial main connections to the overall faith family, God built deep relationships between Min and other students and adults. Once she graduated from high school, she served as an intern with the church youth ministry for a summer and teamed more closely with the youth volunteers and pastoral staff. Now that Min is a young adult, she is leading multiple medical mission trips with the church and helping launch a new ministry to college students.

Not just Danny but the entire church community (with an extra boost from that camp speaker) expanded Min's vision for a character-rich faith that focused on others, not just herself.

For Min and the rest of this generation, character is not just conceived, it's received.

As teenagers live out Jesus' goodness every day by loving God and their neighbors, character is not what teenagers dream up in their own minds. Instead, it's what they see and receive from real people and are then inspired to repeat. It's not a passive receiving but an active receiving grounded in trust.

The good news is that, like Danny, you are a key example of character to your students. The problem is that you alone are not enough. You might not be able to invest in particular students as often or for as long as you'd like, which is where community helps fill in those gaps.

As we saw with Min, who needed the example not just of Danny but of the broader church, the selfless character choices inherent in following Jesus run counter to the strands of US culture, especially evident in White contexts, that elevate the individual. Danny was the essential portal to a deeper and wider community that taught and modeled godly character in a collective way. And trust was the portal that opened Min up to that teaching and modeling.

Three Barriers to Cultivating Trust

Our progress in building trust that leads to faith beyond youth group is often hindered by three barriers, two of which relate to this anxious, adaptive, and diverse generation and one of which relates to us.

1. Young People Don't Trust Institutions, Including the Church

Across nations and generations, distrust has become the norm. In one worldwide study of twenty-eight countries, 59 percent of the thirty-six thousand respondents of diverse ages admitted their default is "distrust until I see evidence that something is trustworthy."[6]

The same global study highlights the trust gap between socioeconomic statuses. Those from lower income levels are an average of fifteen points lower in trust levels than those from higher income levels.[7]

One teenager talked about being "proud of my church" because of the ways members have tried to build trust with young people who have had bad experiences with church in the past. "I love how I know I can invite them to our church, because our church gives people a space when they have been hurt by the church to come back from that and recover. My personality has been shaped by the safe space here that I can now share with others. I've informed so many people who aren't Christian at my school about what being a Christian is, and that you shouldn't be hated by people who are Christians. Just so many things that are such misconceptions."

2. Young People Don't See the Church as Relevant or Kind

In a national Springtide survey of diverse thirteen- to twenty-five-year-olds, only 14 percent reported that they trust organized religion completely while 39 percent indicated that they've been harmed by religion.[8]

In the midst of their quest for identity, belonging, and purpose, half of teenagers don't think religious institutions care about what—or who—matters most to them. In the eyes of young people, the largest gaps between the concerns of the church and their own are evident in (listed in order from greatest to smallest) LGBTQ+ rights, gender equity, immigration rights, income inequality, disability rights, environmental causes, reproductive rights, and racial justice.[9]

Of course, these are *personal* priorities to teenagers because they are about *persons* teenagers know and care about—or themselves.

A student shared with us that their friends make narrow assumptions about what church is like based on negative perceptions: "Mostly when people say 'church' they're like, 'Church?' and I'm like 'Yeah, church,' and they're like, 'Oh, it's probably whack for you—you know, so closed off.' They have the most stereotypical version of church. . . . [But here at this church] we talk about so many issues all the time. Because at other churches they don't really. Like, 'LGBT, don't mention it. Don't talk about gun violence. Don't mention Black people.'"

3. Leaders Seek Grand Gestures

Grand gestures are . . . well . . . pretty grand. But monumental relational moves aren't necessarily the best path to trust. As researcher and storyteller Brené Brown advises, "Trust is built in very small moments."[10]

Amy Carnall, a part-time Pennsylvania family pastor and key member of our research team for this project, explains how she helps volunteers build trust through consistency and closeness: "I encourage them to think about trust like a piggy bank. Every time I show up where I say I will be, show my students I like and know them, listen openly, and share honestly, I'm putting a deposit into their trust bank. That bank fills slowly over time."[11]

We interviewed one college pastor serving in a downtown church who confirmed it took lots of ongoing moments of connection for his students to trust him with what mattered most to them. Every week at church, he would invite students out for dinner. Or he would text everyone and ask, "Hey, is anyone down to grab Boba this afternoon?" That time together, and even the act of making the offer repeatedly, showed this college pastor's desire to build relationships and thus built trust.

In addition to time outside of youth group, our research site visits highlighted that when adults remember what a kid has shared with them, they cultivate trust. As one volunteer youth leader in a Reformed church in the upper Midwest recommends, "If a kid shares an important story, ask them follow-up questions about that. If they're really looking forward to an upcoming trip, when they get back, ask them about it. Show them you remember, that you care, that you are interested in what they have to say, and build that relationship with them more than just [during] that hour and a half at youth group."

How Jesus Built Trust with the First Youth Group

We like to think of Jesus' oh-so-willing-but-oh-so-imperfect disciples as the first youth group. Just like yours today, Jesus' band of young people[12] undoubtedly wondered if they could fully trust Jesus—and each other. Perhaps Jesus chose to invest in his most intimate followers as a collective over three years because he knew the power of both consistency and closeness.[13]

Jesus' strategy seems to have worked—unsurprisingly, since it's Jesus. He cultivated such a high trust relationship with his twelve disciples that following his crucifixion and resurrection, almost all were willing to die for him.[14]

While we could point to a host of Scripture passages in which Jesus builds trust through consistency and closeness (Jesus did a lot of eating, walking, talking, and teaching with his followers over those three years), we'll zero in on the trust he cultivates in Matthew 14:22–33. After feeding five thousand men (and probably at least that many women and children), Jesus sends the disciples in a boat across the Sea of Galilee and heads to a nearby mountain to pray.

Before dawn, a storm arises on the sea and batters the disciples' boat. Wanting to help, Jesus walks on the water toward them, but they don't recognize him and mistakenly believe he is a ghost. Lacking neither boldness nor eagerness, Peter leaves the boat and walks toward Jesus—until his fear of the fierce storm causes him to sink. Jesus reaches out his hand to save Peter, and as Jesus and Peter climb into the boat, the wind dies and the whole boatload of disciples worship Jesus.

Empathy.

Literally, *empathy* means "feeling with."

Or as we define it: empathy = noticing + caring.

Noticing is recognizing someone else's emotions.

Caring is responding to those emotions with feelings of our own.[15]

This sort of empathy is the first step toward good ministry. And good parenting. Not to mention good marriage, good friendships, good neighboring, a good life overall . . . and a good faith beyond youth group. If consistency and closeness are the soil of cultivating trust, Jesus planted trust through two crucial seeds that are deeply meaningful to this generation, the first of which was his *empathy*. Even while communing intimately with his Abba Father, Jesus remained aware of what his youth group was navigating. He left what was almost certainly a really good prayer time to help his endangered followers. Furthermore, as Peter's initial faith disintegrated in the face of gusty winds, Jesus showed empathy again when he noticed what was happening to Peter and cared enough to save him.

As a second trust-building seed that connects with a generation hungry for belonging, *authenticity* was shown by Jesus through sharing his true self with his twelve-person group. When the disciples feared the form walking on water was a ghost, Jesus revealed his authentic self by stating, "It is I" (Matt. 14:27). Shortly after, as Peter was drowning in fear (literally!), Jesus grabbed him and shared his authentic feelings about his daring disciple: "You of little faith" (v. 31). Jesus revealed that he could be his followers' source of bravery. (Plus, how very like Jesus to authentically comment on Peter's "little faith" only *after* he'd grabbed hold of Peter.)

Navigational Tools for Cultivating Trust

"I like to think that if Jesus walked the earth today, he'd spend a lot of time at seventh-grade tennis matches."

At age seventy-one, "Slick" (as everyone calls him) no longer volunteers as a small group leader at his church. Realizing that he'd rather get to know "all the kids," Slick, along with the youth pastor and other volunteers, has helped create a trust-filled culture where every kid feels known and welcomed.

Prior to COVID-19, the local McDonald's was the youth group hangout. When the fast-food restaurant closed its dining room during the pandemic, Slick bought a used limo so he could take groups of students through its drive-thru for milkshakes.

Nearly every person we met at this church told us Slick is core to their youth ministry, in part because he visits youth group graduates who attend colleges within driving distance. According to Slick, "When I visit, if the kids have half as much fun as me, then it's a success. But you have to build a relationship with college students before they are in college. If I just called up these kids to visit, they would think I was a creeper or something."

Thanks to Slick's generous love for others, one young adult at the church labeled Slick the "hands and feet of Jesus." Another young person described Slick as setting "the standard for who we are as a church . . . how we care about each other, support each other, and encourage each other in all aspects of life."

Through his closeness and consistency, Slick is able to cultivate trust and inspire the entire church toward more Christlike character. Just like Slick embodies the empathy and authenticity we see in Jesus, you and your community can too.

Slick sometimes gets "ghosted" (that was the term he used!) by students. While that can feel like rejection to any adult, Slick notices the kids who ghost him and cares enough not to do the same. He believes that "[even when] you get ghosted by the kids . . . you can never ghost them back."

He went on to describe why. "When a kid ghosts me, there's usually a reason behind it. That kid is hurting and needs to know I still care." Even more broadly, Slick explained what motivates him to build relationships with diverse teenagers. "Some are easy to hang out with, and some aren't. It's the ones who aren't as easy to hang out with who really need a friend."

Based on the example of Slick and other amazing adults we met at every ministry we visited, we suggest *two empathetic habits* that cultivate greater trust: listening and nonjudgmental prompts.

Cultivate Trust through Listening

"Being heard is so close to being loved that for the average person, they are almost the same."[16] When our friend Mike Park, a church-planting pastor in New York City, shared this quote with a group of youth leaders at one of FYI's innovation summits, the room fell quiet. In the midst of all we do to try to build faith beyond youth group, if we aren't creating relational spaces and places where young people feel heard, we are likely wasting our time.

One year before we visited a nondenominational church focused on cultivating character in all generations, one of its active members—sixteen-year-old Emma—was suffering from heightened anxiety and depression. Desperate for any sort of relief, Emma tried to end her life by suicide.

One of the first people Emma called when she began thinking of suicide was Nicole, her small group leader. Emma knew that Nicole would be a nonjudgmental and unanxious presence who would listen to her in her pain.

At Nicole's insistence, Emma told her parents and started meeting with a mental health professional. Emma's doing better now, and Nicole's listening and support have been pivotal in Emma's improved mental health.

Faith Beyond Youth Group in Real Life: An Interview with Jonathan Banks

As part of our research, the Fuller Youth Institute awarded subgrants to seven amazing ministries so they could apply the character compass to their contexts. Led by COO Jonathan Banks, Urban Outreach Foundation (UOF), whose mission is to promote healthy churches, excellence in leadership and preaching, and community development, is one of those grantees.

UOF leveraged their funding to launch YOUniversity, a faith-based leadership development approach with online training for tweens, teens, and young adults as well as for parents and youth leaders. They were committed to cultivating trust with young people from the very beginning.

Jonathan, can you please tell us a bit more about YOUniversity?

Our team describes YOUniversity as "God's way to lead with purpose and passion." It's focused on Black young people and Black churches. African Americans often view themselves as resource-constrained and rightly believe good leaders will give their community access to resources. We want the YOUniversity curriculum to help young people grasp that leadership isn't about position. It's about character and a lifestyle of influence.

How have you earned the trust of the young people involved in YOUniversity?

Fundamentally, we listened to them. As we developed our curriculum, we hosted listening sessions with over one hundred Black teenagers from churches in four different US cities. When we started each session, we told them that their words had the potential to affect thousands of young people. In every city, we said the same thing: "If you help us by sharing your thoughts and experiences, we can help other young people like you."

Why has listening to young people been so important in creating YOUniversity?

I believe in listening to all generations, especially young people. But listening wasn't my goal. Listening has been important because it's a requirement for my ultimate goal, which is to cocreate character-building resources with young people. Listening is a key step toward my goal of doing ministry *with* young people and not *for* them.

What did you learn from what teenagers had to say?

Well, first off, we shortened the name. We had been calling it "Champion YOUniversity," but they liked "YOUniversity" better. They are right. It's a better name.

Listening to actual teenagers also helped us understand what keeps them from leading. They aren't afraid to lead; what they lack is a path they can follow. Young people in communities that are resource-deprived or on the margins of our society are ready to grow in character; they just need a map.

Jonathan, before leading UOF, you were a pastor. What advice would you give a leader who wants to listen better and cultivate trust with young people?

Just like kids smell fear, kids smell insincerity. So, if you're not ready to really listen, or you're not equipped to listen without preconceived views of youth, don't pretend like you are.

Plus, sometimes you're not the best person to be asking the questions. Wise youth leaders sometimes need another trusted adult to ask their teenagers questions like: What do your youth leaders not get about you? What do your youth leaders do that makes you feel seen and heard? How can your leaders help you grow even closer to God?

Asking teens for input and insight in ways that make them feel valued and that they have agency is crucial. Such critical listening takes courage, intentionality, and vulnerability. But without it, our work can feel like just another exercise in teens being disingenuously invited to share their hearts with zero likelihood of it making a difference that is meaningful to them. As one eighteen-year-old told us during one of our listening sessions, "Being here made me feel like I mattered . . . like we are heard as people of color. That we matter and that there are actually people here to help us in this world."

To find out more about YOUniversity and Urban Outreach Foundation, visit UrbanOutreachFoundation.com.

Cultivate Trust through Nonjudgmental Prompts

Regardless of how gently we try to ask a question, it can still feel like an accusation in the ears of young people. Based on our understanding of the synergy between empathy and trust, we encourage you to replace questions with short conversation prompts.

One of my (Kara's) favorites is "I'm curious . . ." In the past, I might have asked a teenager, "How do you align your ongoing drinking with what Scripture says about how God wants us to treat our bodies?" Now I try to be more empathetic by nudging: "I'm curious how you align your ongoing drinking with what Scripture says about how God wants us to treat our bodies."

It's softer. And gentler.

Some of my other favorite nonjudgmental prompts are:

"I wonder . . ."

"I'm guessing that . . ."

"I can imagine that . . ."

"It might be that . . ."

And the ever useful, "Tell me more . . ."

Authenticity

When it comes to discipling young people, it's important not to pretend to be someone you're not. In fact, Slick is a great example of just that. With a frequent self-deprecating chuckle, Slick made multiple comments during our interview like "I'm no scholar," "I'm no theologian," "I'm no preacher," and in describing himself as a teenager, "I was no angel."

As a self-designated "grandfather" to the kids in the church, Slick knows it's best to be his authentic self around teenagers. "I just like hanging out with kids. I just act like my goofy self." Minutes later, Slick clarified, "I don't have all the answers. I just hang out with teenagers."

At another church located over a thousand miles from Slick's church, which our research team also visited, the youth pastor confirmed the power of authentic leaders who develop authentic relationships: "Young people can *smell fake* a mile away." He continued, "I tell leaders to be themselves. Kids might think you're uncool. But what's most important is to *be who you are*."

One thousand-member northeastern church we visited so valued a culture in which people could authentically be themselves that one of its young adults said the church is the reputed "bad boy" of their denomination. As characterized by one high school student during a focus group, "When I walk into our Sunday school, I see people I've never met in my life who heard about our church . . . and are drawn to our 'come as you are' approach. I've seen people walk in wearing anything from fancy suits to football jerseys. Our church is very open and inviting."

Whether we wear suits, football jerseys, or something in between, our research suggests you and I can cultivate trust as we *authentically share three aspects of who we are*: our generation, our ethnicity or culture, and our mistakes.

Authentic about Our Generation

Leaders cultivate trust when they act their own age and are aware of how their generational distinctives affect how they build character and faith.

During our season studying a predominantly Chinese congregation and its pursuit of character, the church hosted a multigenerational retreat. During the weekend, young people courageously shared how the questions adults asked them at worship services and church events bothered them. Two questions were particularly irksome: "Are you hungry?" and "Are you dating anyone?" As one college student explained, "Those questions feel so intrusive to me. They prevent me from inviting friends to come to this church."

After listening to young people's concerns, a fifty-year-old stood and explained, "It never occurred to us that those questions would be off-putting to you. We ask if you're hungry because we want to take care of you physically. We ask about dating because we want you to be in meaningful community. Those questions are our way of showing our support."

After more dialogue, a young person stood and used the same phrasing as the fifty-year-old: "*It never occurred to us* that that's why you were asking those questions. My friends and I thought you were just getting into our business."

By authentically sharing their own experiences and preferences, both sides of the generational divide agreed to try to do what was best for the other. Adults committed to ask fewer questions, and young people pledged to not be so annoyed when they did.

Authentic about Our Ethnicity or Culture

It quickly became obvious as we visited diverse congregations that adults can cultivate trust when we are authentic about our own background, culture, and ethnicity and see those factors as influences on the way we live our faith and do ministry.

Ministries build trust when their leadership reflects the ethnicity and culture of those in their community whom they feel called to serve. Pastors strengthen trust when they don't pretend to "get it" when someone uses a cultural reference they've never heard before.

Volunteers build trust by not pretending they understand someone else's cultural or ethnic experience just because they have a few friends from similar backgrounds. Small group leaders cultivate trust by resisting stereotypes and avoiding assumptions in their remarks about students' experiences.

Leaders build trust by doing work to learn about and lament historical and current practices undergirded by racism and White supremacy that have caused harm and injustice across cultures and generations. Faith communities develop trust when they authentically acknowledge and celebrate the cultures represented in their church and community.

For example, one of the multiethnic churches we studied hosts an annual international food festival. Every year, church members from South America, Africa, the Caribbean, and Europe dress up in clothing that represents their cultures of origin and demonstrate dance and other rituals. The biggest highlight is usually the food representing different traditions (accompanied by heaps of friendly trash talk about which dish is "the best"). As the pastor of this church explained, "Sure, we are a little competitive about our favorite foods. But seeing our different cultures helps us love each other as brothers and sisters."

Authentic about Our Mistakes

"Diverse and safe."

When I (Kara) and a few other members of our research team visited a dynamic multiethnic church to understand how it formed character, those were the two dominant adjectives teenagers used to describe their youth ministry.

Part of what made the youth ministry so safe is that its small group leaders have made two commitments: to come every week and to share not just their spiritual highs but also their spiritual lows. In our research focus groups and in conversations, students expressed gratitude that their small group leaders discussed the mistakes they made in the past—and continue to make today. Learning about their mentors' struggles helped students realize it's all right for them to struggle, or as this church proclaims in one of its mantras, "It's okay not to be okay."

These leaders' openness to sharing their struggles also opened doors for students to give more of themselves. During the pandemic, Ethan's group of tenth-grade boys switched from meeting in person to meeting on Zoom. At the end of one small group, Ethan asked the boys to share prayer requests and then prayed for each request. As the other boys were logging off, Brandon, a student in the group, asked if Ethan could stay online for a few minutes.

Ethan replied, "Sure," figuring that Brandon wanted to share something he didn't feel comfortable discussing with the others. But Brandon went a different direction. "Ethan, I noticed you didn't share any prayer requests. *How can I be praying for you?*"

Deeply touched, Ethan shared about a challenge he was facing at work, which prompted Brandon to bow his head and pray aloud for Ethan.

It was initially Ethan's closeness and consistency, along with his empathy and authenticity, that helped him grow closer to Brandon at the speed of trust. That trust opened additional doors for Ethan to mentor Brandon and shape his character.

REFLECTION QUESTIONS

1. This chapter shared findings from one study indicating that only 1 out of 10 US young people received contact from a leader from any faith (not just Christianity) during the first year of the pandemic. What thoughts or feelings does that spark in you?

2. That's the bad news. Here's the good news: 70 percent of the young people surveyed said they value relationships even more now. What ideas or emotions does that raise for you?

3. Do you agree that you can cultivate character and faith beyond youth group at the speed of trust? Why or why not?

4. Three trust-eroding barriers were identified: young people don't trust institutions, including the church; young people don't think the church is relevant or kind; and we leaders seek grand gestures. Which of these three is most likely to hinder you from cultivating character-building trust with teenagers?

5. As you build empathy with teenagers, do you need to develop better listening skills, better nonjudgmental prompts, or both? In what sorts of situations with students do you want to be more empathetic?

6. As you grow in showing your true self to young people, do you need to focus more on being authentic about your generation, your ethnicity or culture, or your mistakes? In what youth ministry situations do you want to be more authentic?

FIVE

MODEL GROWTH
Everyday Faith Starts with You

Teenagers can tell when something is phony. If you're saying all the right things but kids know that you're holding a grudge, that speaks to them louder than whatever else you said about forgiveness. I think when kids see adults modeling things that are really hard or challenging or outside the norm, it creates room for them to feel like, "It's okay for me to do this because I know my leader has tried this before."

Gabe is a volunteer with high school ministry at my (Brad's) church. After his thirty-ninth birthday last September, he committed to training to run a 400-meter race competitively again before turning forty. Gabe had run the 400 in high school and college, and while he'd stayed active, he was nowhere near his former speed.

Determined to work toward his goal, Gabe started showing up to the track early on the weekends to train. He reflected, "It was humbling. But I knew it was good for my body and good for my mind and spirit. So I kept at it." As the year stretched on, "It got real." He signed up for a race. He started working with a personal trainer. As a fourth-grade teacher and father of two elementary-aged kids, he didn't always have much bandwidth for training, so sometimes he settled for workout videos at home. Alongside training, he changed his diet, visited a chiropractor, and even went to cryotherapy. (I had to look that up—it involves ice!)

On May 1, Gabe raced the 400 competitively again. He finished just nine seconds slower than his college speed. And he was four months ahead of turning forty.

While this was something to celebrate, it wasn't the most important part of his experience. Reflecting on the eight-month journey, Gabe shared, "I ran today for myself, which is new." It was no longer about proving himself or being good enough for others' expectations, which had fueled his running as a teenager. "I enjoyed it when I was younger but was always anxious about what it might mean if I wasn't winning." At the same time, he wanted to do this not only for himself but also "to spark anyone to do something for themselves and see it through. I am thankful that God made me the way he did and that God makes me new every day."

Gabe's commitment and follow-through were inspiring not only to our young athletes but to everyone in our youth ministry. One student commented, "It was cool to see him go for something he really wanted to do, and put in the work, and actually reach his goal." He was modeling growth.

How We Model Matters

Whatever our goals, our real lives reflect something to our students. The question is, What are we reflecting? Is it a gospel-shaped life? Is it beautiful because it radiates good news (Isa. 52:7)? Are we reflecting a life worth following? Worth repeating?

What Is Modeling?

We define *modeling* as *showing others who we are every day*. Today's anxious, adaptive, and diverse teenagers wonder: *Are you for real? Are you the same outside church as you are inside?*

They're watching, and our actions either build or break down the trust we talked about in chapter 4. When we live consistently, we let them know they can trust us with the parts of themselves they might be hesitant to bring to church—including their doubts, questions, mistakes, and hurts.

Leaders today can model consistency and integrity as they live everyday faith imperfectly, both in and beyond church. In this way, our ministries become communities of practice (which we'll explore more deeply in chapter 7) and growth.

Character Is Caught before It's Taught

Modeling comes before teaching in the way we've oriented the Faith Beyond Youth Group Compass because research across multiple disciplines affirms that character, like so much of discipleship, is typically "caught" before it's "taught."[1] If you think back on your own experiences, you'll likely remember people in your life who demonstrated a particular virtue, whether or not they talked about it.

For example, I have a friend who grew up in South America in a home where hospitality was so common that it was just a given. Her parents frequently welcomed kids or adults who needed somewhere to stay—sometimes short-term, sometimes long-term. This type of compassionate hospitality was such a way of life for her family that she was shocked to learn as a young adult that other households found it unusual. For the decade I've known this friend, she and her husband have often welcomed in friends as well as strangers, helping their own kids "catch" what she caught from her parents: Welcome as a way of life. Compassion as commonplace.

Once you've caught a lesson like that, teaching might reinforce it, give language to explain it, or help you interpret your experience. But it's already inside you.

Four Barriers to Modeling Growth

Unfortunately, there are barriers that prevent young people from accessing adults who model growth. Let's look at four prominent ones.

1. Young People Can't Be What They Can't See

There's a difference between being a *role model* and *modeling growth*. A role model is an inspirational figure, an ideal, someone to imitate.[2] But the emphasis is on the cultural influence of the model, not necessarily their character. Role models may be distant; we call athletes, leaders, or performing artists role models when their social status elevates their actions, but kids don't actually know them personally. Not only might role models be distant but they also often fall from their proverbial pedestals—usually for the types of character gaps we lamented in chapter 2. They fail to hold the standards we expect, sometimes in epic proportions. They don't live up to the hype. Disappointment over failed role models can leave young people disoriented and cynical.

> "It's hard to be what you can't see." —Marian Wright Edelman, founder and president emerita of Children's Defense Fund[3]

In contrast, a *growth model* is closer in proximity, is in relationship with a young person, and ideally gives them a real-time view of a life in progress. Adult models can be especially powerful for young people who haven't seen people who look like them or share their background hold positions of power and influence. This happens with Indigenous young people who haven't seen their elders represented in government. It happens with Black, Latina/o, and Asian young people who read only schoolbooks written by White authors. It happens to any first-generation college student who has to learn the ins and outs of complicated systems on their own.

And it happens with young women . . . everywhere. For many, the experience strikes most painfully in their churches. Even when women's leadership gifts are affirmed in theory, sometimes women are not free to exercise those gifts in practice. In my (Brad's) own tradition, the Church of the Nazarene, there was a higher percentage of ordained women in the early 1900s than there is today—by almost triple.[4] That means it's less likely for a teenager now to be growing up in a church with a female pastor than it was one hundred years ago. It's hard to be what you can't see. Especially when you *can* imagine it, but systemic bias and power limit real-life examples.

I (Kara) first felt God calling me to full-time vocational ministry when I was sixteen. While I had all sorts of male pastors affirm that calling, I didn't know of many female pastors. I needed a live visual aid—a pastor who was a woman—for me to have a picture of what my future life might look like.

Then God connected me with a female youth leader—in a church bathroom, of all places. I was visiting another church for a citywide youth event, and as I was washing my hands in the women's restroom, I met a youth pastor from another church. She handed me her business card, and I met with her several times over the next ten years. Each time, I received another piece to the puzzle of my calling as my passion grew to see more adults love and serve young people.

2. We've Segregated the Church by Age

I (Brad) was recently listening to a podcast episode that featured a coal miner from Alabama. He was a union laborer, telling the story of how his career started a dozen years ago. What stood out to me about this interview was his reflection that one of the most valuable features of his job was listening to the "old hands," the seasoned miners who had spent a lifetime doing the work, training up younger apprentices, and changing with the industry.[5]

Few fields of work still lean on this sort of apprenticeship approach. The church could be one of them—but often is not.

For decades now, we've segregated the church by age for the majority of our programming and community life. This arrangement may seem convenient to adults and might even be preferred most of the time by children and youth, but it prevents all of us from regularly interacting with other generations. That's a problem for modeling.

In contrast, our own FYI Sticky Faith research found that intergenerational relationships are one of the keys for developing lifelong faith in young people. Specifically, young people's connection with other generations in corporate worship, mentoring relationships (formal or informal), and even contact after high school from an adult outside the youth ministry all correlate with faith beyond youth group.[6]

What's more, our Growing Young research found that young people stay engaged with church when they experience "keychain leadership," which is marked by shared authority and meaningful "load-bearing" work in the congregation. In some of our research visits to congregations nationwide, we heard stories a lot like the coal miner's about young people learning the ropes of ministry and being apprenticed in hands-on service.[7]

An older Latina church leader shared her church's recipe for nurturing young leaders, tying it clearly to belonging: "Part of belonging is serving. Instead of saying, 'No, no, you're too young,' we say, 'Do you want to be involved?' We give lots of on-the-job training. Then they do ministry and see change happen, which raises their excitement. They participate and see the fruit."

3. We've Outsized Extroversion

Unfortunately, we too often model a Christianity that confuses extroversion with faithfulness, spirituality, and even good character.[8] Charisma goes a long way in church circles. This is no secret and echoes back long before the church's origins. A charismatic leader draws people in, inspires, and garners a following. Unfortunately, we easily conflate charisma with character.

What we talk about far less often is the outsized role of extroversion in the church. Despite the church being one body with many gifts (1 Cor. 12), extroverts come with the gifts congregations seem to prefer. Being an extrovert who has held a lot of church leadership roles, I (Brad) know this all too well. Most church environments were made for people like me: those comfortable in groups of all sizes, quick to speak up, willing to either share spontaneously or prepare for public speaking as the situation requires, energized by "people time," and happy to engage in small talk with acquaintances or strangers (okay, so I don't love that last one, but otherwise I mostly fit this bill). We're not only exhausting for those who are more introverted by nature but actually set up unrealistic norms for everyone.

Youth ministry follows this pattern to extremes.

Churches and parachurch ministries prefer youth leaders who embody what Mark DeVries calls the "youth ministry superstar," someone who is dynamic, committed, magnetic, relational, creative, organized, and a great communicator.[9] Several of these qualities are animated by extroversion.

With leaders like this, it's no wonder youth group is for extroverts. One White leader in our interviews shared, "A lot of our students feel like to be a disciple, they've got to be outgoing, or they've got to be willing to be on a stage, or they've got to be a good speaker, or they've got to be charismatic. And I have tried to let students know that that is just a small subset of giftedness."

This set of assumptions makes young people feel unwelcome if they lean quieter, prefer smaller groups or one-on-one conversations, get drained by lots of people interactions, or have social anxiety. Or if they just don't think extroverts are listening to them very well.[10]

According to researcher Susan Cain's work on introverts, when you're modeling extroversion as the favored norm in your ministry, you're likely missing one in three students.[11]

4. We've Confused Influence with Being Influencers

Today I (Brad) am writing on the sidelines of a soccer tournament. A few yards away, two middle school girls are working hard to imitate a TikTok dance in front of a smartphone. Eventually, they'll be satisfied with their recording and submit their offering to the judgment of the virtual world. I don't know them, so I have no idea if this is just a fun way to burn time between games, a creative hobby, or part of a hope that they'll get their shot at celebrity.

Kids now know about "influencers" from a young age. Preschoolers pose for the camera and ask later whether anyone commented. Elementary-aged kids follow YouTubers who stream gaming sessions. By the time kids hit middle school, they're typically immersed in the world of influencer culture, flooded with models of all kinds.

Celebrity is everywhere and seemingly open-access—at least in young viewers' minds. The teenager nearest you can probably rattle off a handful of influencers you've never heard of whose followers on a given platform number in the millions.

Celebrity has always been fleeting; today's celebrity is mind-spinning.

This might just be amusing if it weren't for the way influencer culture models a whole layer of reasons for a teenager to feel worthless, or at least less than enough, based on some invisible and impossible standard. Comparison eats at almost everyone who participates in social media—if we feel it as adults, we know it's compounded for teens.

While it can be tempting for faith leaders to follow the trends and build "platforms" (and believe me, we feel these pressures with you), it's dangerous to prioritize influence, followers, and reach over ministry to the people actually in front of us—the ones who see how we really live. Most youth ministry is slow and personal. It's not that flashy. As youth pastor and school administrator Steve Dang notes, "We want to be influencers with platforms, but kids actually need people modeling process."

But make no mistake: youth ministry *is* about influence. And in that respect, we follow Jesus' own example of modeling growth.

How Jesus Modeled Growth

Perhaps one of the most surprising features of the Gospels of Matthew and Luke is their inclusion of some form of Jesus' birth narrative. Jesus doesn't arrive on the scene a fully formed human; he starts as a baby, and then he grows up. Luke even famously shares a story of a twelve-year-old Jesus who wanders away from his parents and even questions their rebuke. After this, he "kept increasing in wisdom and stature, and in favor with God and people" (Luke 2:52 NASB).

While Jesus was an influencer of his day, what he modeled was an anti-celebrity trajectory. Henri Nouwen calls it "downward mobility," a selfless path toward others and, ultimately, toward the cross.[12] Even in first-century Palestine, this choice was so countercultural that his closest followers didn't understand his "power move" *away* from power until after his death and resurrection.

After seeing Jesus perform miracle after stunning miracle, his disciples must have wondered, *Is this guy for real?* They must have questioned if Jesus' standard was perfection, or at least total awesomeness. They certainly assumed he would seize religious and political power—and some even believed military might—from the rulers of the day. Imagine their surprise when Jesus turned their assumptions upside down.

Jesus Walked the Talk

Jesus' teachings and way of life were inseparable. He "walked the talk." We have this saying for a reason. It's hard for us to do the same! But Jesus modeled for us what absolute consistency between words and actions can look like. In the words of author Diana Butler Bass,

> [Jesus] invited [disciples] into a way of life based on a vision of a wildly gifting God, who created everything, who turns authority upside down, who shatters the pretenses of power, who proclaims a kingdom of the heart, and who brings the poor, the outcast, the forgotten, and the mourning to a table set with an endless feast. And he taught this by holding forth the rule of love, extending the purview of divine commands, and speaking in proverbs, poetry, paradox, and parables to confound the learned and compel the curious.[13]

As a part of the Trinity, Jesus also modeled connection with God the Father. He frequently practiced worship and prayer, both with others and alone. Communion with God was not something Jesus checked off a list; it was as natural as breathing.

Jesus was "the whole package," *God with us* who lived an integrated faith that both garnered a large following and cost him his life.

Jesus Loved Radically

Jesus modeled *love* more than any other trait. Unconditional love. Patient love. Forgiving love. Radical love.

Jesus' love was expressed through healing, serving, freeing, and truly seeing people others preferred not to see. He touched lepers and threw out demons. In one dramatic story in Mark, he released a man from a "legion" of demons and gave him back his dignity, his humanity, and his right to his own name (5:1–20).

Unafraid of social stigma, Jesus frequented dinner parties with sinners. He calls a desolate woman "daughter" (Mark 5:34) and refuses to accuse a woman who'd been publicly shamed (John 8:11). These stories reveal a Jesus who strips away all the categories that drive distrust, division, and dehumanization.

Jesus' love isn't just charitable—it's unthinkable.

This love compels Jesus all the way to his death. John 13 records the story we call the Last Supper, a Passover meal shared with his closest friends on the night of his betrayal. John ensures we don't miss the motivation: "Having loved his own who were in the world, he loved them to the end" (v. 1).

Jesus precedes the meal by washing the disciples' feet, taking the role of a house servant and again reversing the script of what a leader does. He models servant leadership and then narrates it for them: "Now that I, your Lord and Teacher, have washed your feet, you also should wash one another's feet. I have set you an example that you should do as I have done for you" (vv. 14–15).

In liturgical traditions, Thursday of Holy Week is called Maundy Thursday because at this final meal, Jesus gives a new "mandate" for his followers both then and now. "A new command I give you: Love one another. As I have loved you, so you must love one another. By this everyone will know that you are my disciples, if you love one another" (vv. 34–35). Radical love is to be our way of life too, and the world will know *who* we are *when* we model it.

Jesus' Life Was—and Is—Worth Imitating

The earliest Christians had a lot to say about modeling their lives after Jesus. Admonitions to imitate Christ are scattered among the letters the first leaders wrote to new believers, which now make up our New Testament epistles. Here are a few:

Follow my example, as I follow the example of Christ. (1 Cor. 11:1)

Whoever claims to live in [Jesus] must live as Jesus did. (1 John 2:6)

To this you were called, because Christ suffered for you, leaving you an example, that you should follow in his steps. (1 Pet. 2:21)

Follow God's example, therefore, as dearly loved children and walk in the way of love, just as Christ loved us and gave himself up for us as a fragrant offering and sacrifice to God. (Eph. 5:1–2)

The very term *Christian* was given to believers as a designation that they were "little Christs," emulating his way in the world.[14] There's no better model today for those of us who want to lead young people toward the fullest possible life than Jesus' own.

Navigational Tools for Modeling Growth

With Jesus' example as their ultimate inspiration, the leaders we interviewed and watched in action gave us plenty of examples of modeling growth to share with you. Following is a list of navigational tools you can use to boost the power of modeling in your ministry.

Increase Proximity + Time

It's hard to overemphasize how much the effectiveness of modeling depends on adults sharing time and space with young people. Similar to the first point on the Faith Beyond Youth Group Compass of cultivating trust, little else is as effective as being in the same spaces—opening homes to one another, going to students' games and performances, and crossing paths in the same neighborhoods. In that vein, the more lives overlap, the less we can choose *not* to model. Students see the good, the bad, and the real. In other words, *shared proximity and time will result in modeling*, like it or not.

In our research, leaders spoke often about the kinds of relationships that grow out of lots of shared experiences over time. One Latina young adult reflected about her experience growing up surrounded by models at her multiethnic church, "Let's say I had class with this adult and he saw me grow up. It's kind of like, 'Well, you're practically my daughter. I've seen you every weekend for the past ten years, so I'm going to tell you if you're not going down the right path or if you need to be put in check.' It's more of an aunt or uncle type of relationship."

We also heard repeatedly in our research about high school students and young adults who actively reach out to younger kids and serve in children's and youth ministry, increasing their proximity to younger generations. One leader mused, "You don't stay connected to people you aren't around anymore. So watching [the former students] be the people who have taken the time out to invest in young people and to teach them [is really gratifying]." It also keeps young adults connected with church after high school.

Sharing proximity and time can be a challenge for today's busy leaders and students. We might be hesitant to ask already-stretched volunteers for more of their precious hours. Here are a few ideas for addressing this challenge with your team:

- Create a shared spreadsheet or calendar where students' activities can be added and updated each season. For example, key sports games, theater or music performances, big school events, and birthdays. Include a column (or another way) for volunteers or staff to indicate who can attend. Circulate this regularly as a way to ensure coverage, and encourage leaders to utilize these opportunities to model showing up for what matters to students. You and your team can invite other students to come with you to these events—increasing the relational touch points of your ministry and the size of the crowd cheering for your students.

- Match up intergenerational prayer partners. Faith Reformed Church in West Michigan wanted every student in the church to have a prayer partner who was actively praying for them. We heard stories of many of these relationships growing far beyond solely praying for students to include other forms of support and investment.

- Within the bounds of your ministry safety policy, invite students along to do "normal life" things together. For example, take a couple of students with you to the grocery store, to run errands, or to exercise. The modeling they'll see in your everyday interactions with others will speak volumes about your own discipleship.

Self-Assess What You're Modeling

How would your students describe your character? What are the qualities and traits you model most? It's helpful to think about this in a few categories:

- *Language.* What words come out of your mouth when you aren't specifically teaching or leading? For example, when you're in casual conversation, driving, texting, or posting on social media. Pay attention for a few weeks to what you say in front of students. What are you modeling with your words?

- *Tech use.* How do you use digital technology, especially your cell phone and social media? What kinds of boundaries do you model? What do students learn from how often you look down at your screen while you're around them, what platforms you're active on, and what you share in images and videos?

- *Work and rest.* Do your students think you work all the time, or do they see you practice rhythms of work and rest? If weekends are workdays for you as a ministry leader, do you take another Sabbath day during the week? Do you answer texts at all hours of the day and night, or do you model ignoring your phone during meals and late in the evening?

- *Loving neighbors.* Do students see you actively loving neighbors, whether through acts of compassion, participation in justice-seeking, extending hospitality, or in other ways?

- *Bouncing back.* Do you model growth from mistakes and failure? Modeling isn't about being perfect.

Admittedly, this sounds good until you're going through it personally. Students will see you make mistakes, and they will likely see you fail. What happens *after* these experiences is sometimes more influential than the mistakes themselves.

Modeling growth also means sharing about how we change over time. Sometimes in conversations with my (Brad's) young adult daughter about a particular social issue, she will say something to the effect of, "But you changed. You didn't used to think that way." And she's right.

Sharing how we've changed our thoughts or beliefs over the years is important because it can be freeing for young people. They see an adult modeling growth by looking back and admitting, "I used to believe ____. Now I believe ____." This grants them permission to be people who grow and change too. They don't have to remain entrenched in the strong opinions they hold today if tomorrow brings new information, new stories, or new relationships that open them to seeing the world and their faith anew.

Be Appropriately Vulnerable

"This is the first time I've ever seen a male pastor cry. I think I needed to see that in real life—that pastors are people too. And that us guys, especially Asian American guys, have emotions, and it's okay to show them."[15]

Our FYI colleague Giovanny Panginda spent hours working on a retreat talk he was giving as a guest speaker. He meditated on a Bible passage, journaled, prayed, and searched for relatable illustrations. He practiced his delivery and timing.

But none of that turned out to be what was most important to the students.

What really opened up conversations that weekend? Gio's vulnerable sharing and his tears. The teaching was focused on Christ and identity, and Gio's own story about his identity journey through tragic loss modeled that it's okay to share struggles—and it's okay to cry.

Gio reflected afterward,

> As leaders, we might find ourselves investing so much time on our sermons that we forget *we* are often our students' primary models of learning. Don't get me wrong—preaching and teaching are very important! But to our students, the way we live out our lives is the greatest sermon we will ever preach because our students are paying close attention to how we talk, what we share, how we react, and especially how we treat others.[16]

Vulnerability can be tough for leaders. But students want us to go there. Within appropriate boundaries, talk about the hard things. The hurt and suffering you've experienced can humanize you for students.

If you're seeing a therapist, let students know. If you've struggled with rejection, share it.

One student from our research described how her small group leader modeled vulnerability: "We would have discussions about struggles and what was going on in our lives, and she was very open. I liked that about her. She was open with how she approached these situations herself in high school, how she reacted, and how she grew from the decisions she made. She was very open with her life, with how she saw the world. The more we share our imperfections, the more we'll learn from them."

Of course, we need to gauge the appropriateness of what we share based on our context, the age of our students, and what kinds of experiences may be triggering for others. Sensational stories about past sins can also have unintended consequences and may actually sound more like bragging than vulnerability. Here's a good general rule: if you're wondering if a personal story might go too far, tell the story ahead of time to another trusted adult in your ministry (or your supervisor) and get feedback before you share with students.

Or follow Jen's advice to her leaders: (1) Tell the story but skip the details. Details get you into trouble. (2) Before you tell it, think about whose benefit you're telling it for. If it's for your own benefit, skip it. If you're trying to get it off your chest or even get a laugh, skip it. Find a safe adult or small group where you can be an adult and share as vulnerably as needed.

Invite Students to Reflect on Their Models and Mentors

Whether in a group reflection, journaling, or one-on-one mentoring, ask young people to reflect on who has modeled growth to them and also to note the social location of those models. With older teenagers, ask questions like these:

- Which teachers, coaches, or other adults do you admire the most and why?
- Which peers do you admire and look up to for how they live their lives?
- Looking at this list, what are the race, ethnicity, and gender of the people you look up to or admire? Are they in the same groups as you? If not, where can you find models with a similar background? Why might this be helpful?

- If all the people on your list share your background, what would you gain from having more models with different backgrounds? Are there any adults you could ask to help you with this?
- How have your parents modeled growth to you? When have your parents (or other family members) admitted they've changed their mind about something? What can you learn from that?
- What does this list of people tell you about your own values?

Help Students Exchange Negative Models for Christ-Centered Ones

Gio relayed a conversation from that same retreat with a student who was struggling with his body image. Gio asked the student to name two of his models, and the young man cited the captain of his wrestling team and a bodybuilder he followed on social media. According to the student, these men had a physique that commanded respect and prestige. Gio asked how the models might be having a negative impact, and the student responded, "The captain of the wrestling team is popular, but he doesn't really know I exist. We're not friends, so I feel like I have to get strong and ripped just to be at his level and get noticed. And the bodybuilder doesn't even know me."

Gio wondered aloud with the student, "Who do you know is strong, has a good physique, but has a healthier view of body image? Who embodies both the faith and the healthy lifestyle you would most like to have?"

The student was able to identify his youth pastor, who also worked as a physical trainer at a local gym. "I like how disciplined he is, going to the gym at 5 a.m. He says he tries to honor God by staying healthy. And the fact that God loves him unconditionally takes the pressure off."

Young people like this one may need to swap their models. In many cases, they need to literally unfollow people on social media who raise their anxiety and lower their self-image. Ask questions like these:

- Who are some of the people you want to be like and why?
- Is there anyone on that list who makes you feel worse about yourself in some way? What do you think are some of the reasons for that?
- Who else could you look to for encouragement or a positive example instead?

Live Everyday Faith, Every Day

"Humility consists in being [in the presence of others] precisely the person you actually are before God." –Thomas Merton[17]

Throughout this book, we're defining *faith beyond youth group* as *Jesus-centered character that matters every day*. And we define *character* as *living out Jesus' goodness every day by loving God and our neighbors*. The "every day" part of both definitions is intentional. We don't get to compartmentalize either faith or character—they don't work that way. In that sense, modeling character for young people sounds a lot like the twentieth-century monk Thomas Merton's understanding of humility. It's being the same person everywhere.

An East Coast church in our study urges their members to "live out the kingdom of God wherever [they] are." In interview after interview, we heard how important it is that faith shape people's lives. The student ministry pastor described her hope for the outcome of their ministry: "Where the rubber hits the road is where it matters. What I'd like to see is all these high school students becoming adults who really do live out the kingdom where they are. Not just a weekend thing, but [young people saying,] 'Wherever I am, whatever college I go to, whatever job I hold, when I have a family of my own, I'm still living out the kingdom wherever I find myself.'"

Our friends at Young Life, one of the resource grant partners we mentioned in chapter 4, may have said it best: "We believe the best discipl*ing* flows out of one's own disciple*ship*." Whatever we share with students comes "out of the overflow" of our own growth.

Faith Beyond Youth Group in Real Life: An Interview with Elizabeth Tamez Méndez

New Generation3 (NG3) is another ministry that, like Jonathan Banks and Urban Outreach Foundation (whom we met in chapter 4), has applied the Faith Beyond Youth Group Compass. Led by founder and executive director Elizabeth Tamez Méndez, NG3 has a mission of "Connecting People—Expanding Perspectives—Shaping the Future."

NG3 produces Spanish and English training, resources, and services that strengthen organizational leadership and intergenerational ministry with multicultural youth and young adults. The NG3 team has utilized the FBYG [Faith Beyond Youth Group] approach to develop a bilingual digital platform and booklet series called JUNTOS: Six Transformational Practices of Latino Churches and Youth.

Elizabeth, when it comes to instilling virtues in young people, why is modeling growth critical?

Young people today are bombarded with fifteen-second sound-bite advice and mirages of "real life" portrayed by social media influencers, but they spend too little time with caring adults to guide them.

Who will help them deal with the tough questions and sort through competing messages? How can they learn to distinguish between constructive and damaging ways of being? How can they learn to hear the Holy Spirit's voice above all others?

Our youth are in need of direction more than ever, and they're hungry for close-knit, transparent, and vested relationships with adults who can inspire them on a faith journey that embodies virtues such as honesty, humility, and perseverance. Modeling is how we show them what it's like to make Christ-reflecting, God-honoring, wise choices that build a healthy *destino*—a direction in life.

What advice would you give leaders and faith communities who want to access the power of modeling to form character?

Power is a perfect descriptor for modeling! Not power in the sense of subjugation or control but rather energy, inspiration, and liberation through healthy relationships. This type of modeling uplifts and helps young people dream dreams for their future, determine the people they want to be, and envision the abundant life Christ offers.

To create this environment, our JUNTOS series offers practical resources and highlights the importance of encouraging your entire congregation to understand and lean into their role as models of growth. JUNTOS is the Spanish word for *together*. Our Christian walk, the shaping of character, and learning to practice virtues all require—by divine design—passing it on from one generation to the next (Deut. 4:9; 6:6–7). Young people learn by observing, reflecting, and doing; they say, "Don't *tell* me, *show* me." When we cultivate close, loving relationships with youth, they can sense our genuine interest, build trust, and give us the privilege of modeling faith and character for them.

You've been working on a character-based project of your own recently; tell us more about your focus and what you've been learning.

Since only about 2 percent of Latina/o congregations have a paid youth minister, our project aims to resource pastors and laity in the church as they lead young people and help shape congregational culture. We've held exploration sessions with pastors, laity, and denominational leaders in different parts of the country. In these conversations, we heard a common need for resources that inspire catalytic conversations, encourage reflective practices, examine culturally and socially relevant issues among Latine[18] youth, and provide practical cues for developing deep relationships with younger generations.

One of the leaders expressed that as Christian congregations, we are missing the opportunity to spark deep conversations about ethics, faith, character, and practicing the virtues that reflect Christ's work within; to promote critical thinking; and to steer away from dogmatic approaches. In response, the JUNTOS series arose!

JUNTOS is the name of our collaborative intergenerational project as well as the framework by which we encourage one another, "rooted and established in love," to grow in faith and "grasp how wide and long and high and deep is the love of Christ" (Eph. 3:17–18).

To find out more about NG3 and the bilingual JUNTOS series, visit NG3Web .org, JuntosSeries.com, and SerieJuntos.com.

Life on Display

Forest Hills Covenant Church is a self-declared "multiethnic, intergenerational, Christ-centered church." They believe their congregation is "giving Boston a taste of the goodness of God," and their youth ministry hopes to provide urban teenagers a safe space for dialogue, empowerment, relationships, and building "an honest, critically thinking, committed relationship with the church and God."

During our research team's visit, we saw leaders model these values over and over. Pastor Christina Tinglof grew up at Forest Hills and has now pastored the community long enough that she's serving the kids of former youth group kids. Students and adults alike overwhelmingly describe her as someone who "truly cares" for people. One youth leader told us that Christina knows what's going on in students' lives because they feel comfortable sharing deeply with her. This trust draws from a long history of building relationships with young people from all kinds of backgrounds, including gang-involved teens.

Pastor Christina both models growth and talks about it. She describes discipleship as "imitating Christ." She wants students to see her imitating Christ, which includes serving in the community and seeking justice. She told us, "I consider social awareness and the pursuit of social justice vital parts of how Jesus lived out his ministry, so that means they should be vital parts of how I imitate Christ in the world. I don't know if the kids could articulate that, but that's what I try to do."

Leaders at Forest Hills describe modeling as their lives "being on display" for students. This intentionality comes through to students and on to their families. One parent described youth ministry as a "safe place" for his kids to discuss problems. Another said the youth group is a place of "no judgment."

Students connect this level of care and welcome with trusting God. A teenager told us about a time when Pastor Christina and other leaders welcomed another teen who was really struggling with his mom's serious health diagnosis and felt distant from God. Because of the leaders' care for that student through such a tough season, the interviewee told us, "It made *me* believe in God way more, made me trust him way more, because there are going to be some of those times where, you know, God isn't there and you're going to feel distant, but it made me believe always to have faith in God."

Every time the youth group meets, they recite their covenant to one another:

> We will treat each other with respect, dignity, and kindness.
>   We will be present to each other.
>   Leaders will be good examples, trustworthy and fun.
>   We commit to a youth group where everyone can be honestly themselves, feel safe, have fun, and grow in their relationship with God.

This is more than a creed—it's a lifestyle. One volunteer serves every week by driving students to youth group. When this volunteer needed to buy a new car, she got a van—not because she needed the extra space herself but to increase her capacity to serve others.

Love modeled like that sticks with a kid. It can inspire the kind of faith that lives long beyond youth group.

REFLECTION QUESTIONS

1. When it comes to character, what do you think is "caught" by young people in your ministry based on the lives of adult leaders?

2. What are some character traits and virtues in your own life that you think are evident to your students?

3. Which of the barriers to modeling growth most impact your teenagers: lack of access to models, segregating the church by age, the outsized importance of

extroversion, or confusing influence with influencer culture?

4. What most inspires you about the life and ministry of Jesus that you want to imitate in your own life and ministry? Who is modeling this kind of leadership for *you*?

5. Who are your students looking to as models outside your ministry? Which of those are positive and which might be negative influences? How could you help young people find healthier, Christ-centered models?

6. What are some ways you can help teenagers think about what they are modeling to their peers and younger kids?

SIX

TEACH FOR TRANSFORMATION

It's Not What You Think

"We don't want to listen to you talk at us."

That's what my student leaders told me (Jen) about six months after I started working at their church. Their comments hurt. Seven years into my youth ministry career, I was confident I knew how to run a ministry. I had a standard formula:

game + three worship songs + twenty-minute talk + small groups = success

As it turns out, my formula—the same model used by virtually every youth pastor I knew—did not work for my students.

After repeatedly telling me they were unhappy only to have their complaints fall on deaf ears, my student leaders approached my boss, the associate pastor, who informed me we needed to meet with these frustrated teenagers. During the meeting, students shared how they didn't want to play "dumb games" or sing songs they didn't know. They wanted to talk about real issues that affected them (like war, divorce, and politics), not the topics (like baptism and the basics of faith) that I thought were critical for their faith formation.

What's more, they wanted to help plan and lead our conversations. They swore that doing so would help them grow in their faith far more than any talk I could give.

As my boss and I later processed the meeting, she affirmed that I knew how to do youth ministry. She also suggested that maybe my knowledge wasn't all that helpful if it didn't connect with the teenagers in our ministry. "What you're doing might be exactly what every other youth ministry in the country is doing," she said. "But if you keep doing it, you're going to lose these kids. Is that what you want?"

Three Barriers to Teaching for Transformation

Of course I didn't want to lose kids. No youth pastor does.

But what if our formula for youth ministry is actually one of the reasons our kids are leaving? What if, far from leading to transformation, our "success" formula is actually stunting young people's spiritual growth?

Faith-based educators are not the only ones trying to discern how best to teach young people. For example, when researchers assessed attention levels in chemistry classes that used three distinct formats (lecture, demonstration, or asking questions), they found college students had fewer attention lapses during demonstrations and questions than during lecture segments.[1]

Similarly, when Scott Freeman, a biologist at the University of Washington, analyzed 225 studies of undergraduate teaching methods, he concluded teaching approaches that "turned students into active participants" reduced failure rates and boosted exam scores by almost one-half a standard deviation.[2] If your statistics knowledge is a bit rusty, trust us when we say that's significant!

Both of these studies suggest that *how we teach* impacts people's ability to learn. Given this, what if we could actually teach in a way that fostered trust with young people so they could catch character and live it out beyond youth group?

Such teaching would truly be transformational. That's why teach for transformation is our third compass point.

Unfortunately, three barriers—our mental models, our misplaced focus, and Gen Z's distrust of authority—often get in the way.

1. Our Mental Models

When I sat down with the students who were frustrated with youth group, I had a picture in my head, a mental model of effective youth ministry. Sadly, my model conflicted with how my students wanted to learn.

For better or worse, we each have a mental model for effective youth ministry, particularly as it relates to teaching. We construct our models based on our own experience, what we're taught about how to do youth ministry, and how others practice youth ministry.

- *Our own experience.* Our own experience in youth group is one of the things that impacts our mental model for teaching in ministry. If you grew up in a ministry where someone gave a talk, chances are that's how you picture youth ministry teaching. In contrast, if you grew up in a more discussion-based ministry, you're likely to default to that as your ministry model. We often aspire to lead the kind of ministry we experienced, not necessarily because we think it results in faith beyond youth group but because it's what we know.

- *What we're taught.* Bible college and seminary classes, as well as popular conference workshops, often focus on "How to Give a Talk That Teenagers Will Listen To," or "Revolutionizing the Youth Ministry Talk," or "Three Things Every Teenager Needs to Hear During Your Talks." Many workshops reduce talks to simple frameworks: share a story, read and explain some Scripture, then tell young people how to apply that Scripture to their lives. While that's a viable format, the prevalence of such workshops makes it seem like effective youth ministry revolves around talking only *at* young people and not *with* them.

- *How others practice youth ministry.* When clips of youth pastor superstars giving sermons routinely show up in our social media feeds and leading curriculum products default to video-driven talks, this, too, reinforces a mental model for teaching centered on sermons. So do books on how to talk to teenagers. Even conversations at network meetings about ideas for talks or strategies for message prep reinforce the idea that *the* way to do youth ministry is by giving a talk.

2. Our Misplaced Focus

We often think our goal in teaching is to transfer information from one person to another. As one youth leader from a diverse Catholic parish in the Chicago suburbs told us, "There's this understanding that you're supposed to know things at a certain age."

Rather than elevating knowledge, Scripture measures fruit by character attributes. "The fruit of the Spirit is love, joy, peace, forbearance, kindness, goodness, faithfulness, gentleness and self-control" (Gal. 5:22–23).

Of course, as youth workers, we know that Christlike character looks like this. According to one youth pastor from a multiethnic small-town congregation, "You know the tree by its fruit. Are teenagers out serving? Are they showing humility? Are they showing compassion? Are they marching in demonstrations? Are they displaying the fruit of the Spirit?"

Unfortunately, rather than recognizing (or even noticing) character traits, we too often praise the kid who finds the Bible passage the fastest. Or the one who can repeat what we said the previous week even though, as another leader admitted, such skills reflect an ability to "regurgitate information" rather than a person's character.

Still another youth leader helpfully summarized that forming character requires shifting our focus from imparting knowledge or "what to think" to training young people "how to think." Leaders from other contexts echoed this, suggesting we need to help teenagers "think for themselves with a theological background." Knowing how to think with a theological background paves the way for young people to leave youth group with Christlike character.

3. Gen Z's Distrust of Authority

Another barrier to teaching for transformation is Gen Z's distrust of authority, which we mentioned in chapter 4. Mental models that assume lecturing (or another one-way transmission of information) are built around the theory that the person talking has some kind of authority that enables them to teach because of their expertise. Young people are often skeptical of this authority because they distrust the institution granting it.

In the same way that they have many internet tabs open simultaneously on their laptops, today's young people can absorb and synthesize various viewpoints and opinions into a mosaic that works for them, and trust themselves to do so. Hearing from only one source makes teenagers wonder what—and who—they are missing, especially since they've grown up in a TikTok world with distributed authority. This diverse generation wants to learn not just from one authoritative source but from many people with differing opinions.

Young people point to adults who share their own stories as more trustworthy. A student in a Midwestern congregation observed, "One thing about having our leaders speak about their experiences and their challenges in life is that we don't realize that they go through the same things we do all of the time, so it really opens our eyes when they say things and tell their stories because we have no idea that they have the same issues. A lot of times we need that reminder that we are not going through things alone." Story sharing leads to trust, which builds authority to speak into young people's lives.

Why Teaching for Transformation Matters

The three barriers we just explored make it difficult to teach for transformation. That's why it is important to remember that adolescents *are* implicitly being taught, formally or informally. According to theologian and ethicist Stanley Hauerwas, "All education, whether acknowledged or not, is moral formation."[3] Our choice isn't whether to do character education but whether or not we're doing it on purpose.[4]

Our team was continually reminded of this as we spoke with youth leaders involved in our research. One priest at a Catholic parish explained, "Everything you do is teaching kids. As soon as kids are pulling in with their families, you are evangelizing. When we gather around the baptismal font, we are evangelizing. When you get into your classroom, you are evangelizing. If you have that mindset, then you start believing that everything you're doing is teaching these kids something good."

To be even more intentional about forming character, theologian Dallas Willard suggested churches need a "curriculum for Christlikeness."[5] Without such intentionality, youth group graduates might leave church knowing *what* they're supposed to believe but not *why* it matters or *how* to live out their faith in their daily lives. They might leave youth group with plenty of knowledge but little that resembles Christlike character.

Similarly, we heard teenagers talk about how it stands out to them when teaching in youth group helps them connect these dots. One student shared that the messages in their youth ministry "are really geared toward our age group and what we might be going through, and they give you a lot to think about and make you consider how your actions toward other people are impacting other people, and how you can better your life and live more through Christ. I feel like those lessons are really important."

Teaching for Transformation Fosters Critical Thinking

Hearing multiple perspectives from different people and inviting teenagers to participate in faith-related conversations teach young people how to think critically about their faith. Like character, we know that *critical thinking* can feel like a loaded term. We, however, define *critical thinking* as *the ability to use your mind to discern and learn.* In doing so, we are loving God with our whole heart, soul, and mind (Matt. 22:37)—an essential part of discipleship.

When adults step back and stop talking, "kids learn to think and ask the right questions to develop ethical reasoning," which lets them catch the Christlike character that leads to faith beyond youth group.[6]

Author Michele Borba provocatively writes, "The best place for kids to learn to speak up and clarify their moral principles is at home, so why not start family disagreements?"[7] We believe another great place for young people to learn to speak up and clarify their moral principles is their faith community, where they are (hopefully) surrounded by adults who model Christlike character and accept them for who they are—even when they disagree.

A multiethnic church in New York experienced the power of this reality firsthand. Both leaders and students from this community affirmed the unique ways in which small groups help young people learn about and practice their character. According to one leader, "We ask each other questions we wouldn't ask otherwise. We encourage everybody in the room to search deep about what's really bothering them and how God can heal that. I don't know if those kinds of conversations are happening in other spaces."

Teaching for Transformation Creates Community

Teaching for transformation also matters because it creates community. Transformational teaching requires deep listening and sharing, two practices that cultivate trust and relationships between people, reinforce teenagers' identity in Christ, and remind them that they belong to God's family. One youth leader from a Latina/o community told us, "I try to make it a relational space rather than 'Hear ye, listen to me because I know so much.'"

Likewise, accompanying young people as they take ownership of their faith forms deep relationships that give teenagers the support they need to practice living out their faith—and character—in the world around them.

One student told us about the power of hearing adults share relationally in small groups. "Before coming to this church, I never really had a connection with an adult or mentor or anything like that. But coming and hearing a small group leader being vulnerable about their struggles—I used to think that adults had everything put together. You turned thirty and you're done, you've figured out all your problems. I was like, 'Oh, well, I guess I've got to wait.' But when I hear leaders here talking about their lives, I'm like, 'Oh, this is normal, okay.' It's a process, it's not going to be over ever."

How Jesus Taught for Transformation

The importance of teaching for transformation is also evident throughout the four Gospels, where Jesus teaches more than he does anything else. In the New Testament, people directly address Jesus about ninety times. He's called *teacher*, *rabbi*, *great one*, or *master* in roughly sixty of those instances—all titles that demonstrate Jesus "lived and died a teacher."[8]

Not only was Jesus recognized as a teacher but he also intentionally used his teaching to transform his first-century followers. Through his teaching, Jesus built trust among his community of followers and modeled growth to them, which we know from chapters 4 and 5 are instrumental in character formation.

Jesus used at least four practices to teach for transformation. He built upon the work of others, told stories, asked questions, and commissioned and shared his authority with his followers.

Jesus Built upon the Work of Others

While Jesus taught as "one who had authority" (Mark 1:22), his place in the Jewish community was evident as he built upon the work of others. Jesus knew and regularly quoted the Hebrew Scriptures. For example, at the start of his public ministry, Jesus quotes Isaiah, saying,

> The Spirit of the Lord is on me,
>> because he has anointed me
>> to proclaim good news to the poor.
> He has sent me to proclaim freedom for the prisoners
>> and recovery of sight for the blind,
> to set the oppressed free,
> to proclaim the year of the Lord's favor. (Luke 4:18–19)

Jesus received both praise and criticism for his deference to the Hebrew Scriptures. In this instance, while some of his listeners spoke well of him, others tried to chase him off a cliff.

Nevertheless, Jesus continued to draw upon the wisdom of others as he taught.

To be clear, what he did is not what we cautioned against at the start of this chapter when we described the danger of constructing a mental ministry model based on how others teach. Jesus did not imitate the teaching of others. He knew his audience and understood the ways in which Jewish teaching was embedded in their everyday lives. Rather than merely copying *how* others taught, Jesus built upon *what* they taught. He expanded it and shared it with his followers in ways that brought new light to it. For example, Jesus frequently built upon the most common interpretations of the Hebrew Scriptures by saying, "You have heard that it was said . . ." (Matt. 5:21) before offering a new, sometimes revolutionary twist to help people better love God and their neighbors. Far from trying to abolish the Hebrew Scriptures, Jesus' new interpretations fulfilled the Law and formed the character of others so that, by imitating Jesus, they could bring God's kingdom to earth (v. 17).

Jesus Told Stories

Jesus also taught for transformation by telling stories, or parables. Such stories invite us to wrestle with and explore their meaning from multiple angles. Author and pastor Diana Butler Bass explains that parables are "mini mysteries. Jesus teaches through detection."[9] Rather than merely transmitting information, Jesus' stories allow us to participate in learning by interpreting them for ourselves using other Scripture passages as well as the wisdom of our tradition and those who have gone before us. They invite us to see ourselves in them, often in ways that change depending on our particular circumstances at the moment. That, in turn, makes stories something we can learn from not just once but time and time again.

Stories are particularly important in character formation because they seldom offer neat solutions. Instead, they give us opportunities to wrestle with moral and ethical dilemmas and empathize with the characters facing them. In particular, Jesus' parables ask us to "dive more deeply into the questions, to wrestle with the parable again and again."[10]

In our research, youth leaders who taught effectively recognized the transformative power of stories in young people. One youth pastor from a nondenominational Chinese American church in Texas explained, "95 percent of the sermons I prepare, my students will not remember. They'll remember the stories I used to illustrate points but not the points." Despite being from a very different context, another youth leader, this one from a mostly White Reformed Church in America congregation in Michigan, relayed that using Scripture as story is far more effective in cultivating character than turning Jesus' stories into "some kind of expository manual."

Teenagers also affirmed the importance of story in their faith formation. One student from a Seventh-day Adventist congregation explained, "It's cool to see how Christianity leads people in their different lives. Leaders always share stories from their personal lives, and it shows me that, through their models, no matter how much adversity you face, God isn't going to leave you."

Jesus Asked Questions

Besides inviting his listeners to participate in stories, Jesus also taught for transformation by engaging people through questions. Jesus asked at least 307 questions that are actually recorded in the Bible.[11] He also fielded an additional 183 questions from other people. Depending on how we count, he answered somewhere between three and eight of those questions. This makes Jesus "almost 40 times more likely to ask a question than he is to give a direct answer."[12]

As much as we might long for Jesus to provide simple, easy answers, he rarely does. Far from being "the answer man," Jesus is instead the great questioner. He knows that questions have the ability to transform us.

I (Jen) have seen this in my own ministry with teenagers. A parent once called me, thrilled because her high school students were regularly talking to her about what we discussed at youth group. Excitedly, she told me, "They always want to know what I think! It's like they leave each week with a question!" She was right. They did. We intentionally sent them out with a question or two to ask at home. As a result, they were ready to continue the conversation with a family member and anyone else who would participate.

Jesus Commissioned and Shared His Authority with Others

After Jesus' ascension, his disciples transformed from cowering behind locked doors to loving others and willingly sharing their faith with the world. Their Christlike character was apparent, often to their own detriment. By living so boldly, they literally changed the world. Their lives showcased the effectiveness of Jesus' teaching.

The disciples' transformation occurred as the result of their very intentional three-year apprenticeship with Jesus, during which he periodically called out their character. Jesus gives Peter a nickname, "rock" (see Matt. 16:18), long before he has done anything to deserve it. This name demonstrates Peter's character. He is trustworthy and solid, a leader who can lay a foundation for others to follow.

Jesus then commissioned his followers and gave them authority. In Luke 10, Jesus sends his disciples out two by two. He empowers them to teach, preach, and cast out demons, a call that he reaffirms at the end of his earthly ministry in Matthew 28. In the same way, young people today long to be part of something bigger than themselves. Like Jesus' disciples, they want to lead and even change their communities. Faith beyond youth group gives them the tools they need to do just that.

Navigational Tools for Teaching for Transformation

If our goal in teaching is to transform teenagers' character and lives, then we have to break free of our old models for youth ministry. Instead, we can build new models that teach for transformation by following Jesus' example and building upon the work of others, telling stories, asking questions, and commissioning and sharing our authority with others. Based on how youth leaders in our research are utilizing these practices, we are confident that teaching like Jesus did will equip students to form habits that will, in turn, shape their character and give them the ability to live out consequential faith.

Use Rituals and Liturgy to Build upon the Work of Others

Teaching for transformation begins just like Jesus began: by building upon the work of others. One way to do this is by utilizing your faith community's liturgies with your teenagers. Now, we know the word *liturgy* can mean different things to different people, but our team believes every faith community has a liturgy. While liturgy in Jen's Episcopal congregation features a formal worship order with hymns, written prayers, lengthy Scripture readings from both the Old and New Testaments, and communion, in Kara's congregation liturgy looks like current worship songs, time to get to know others sitting near you, and an engaging sermon. Brad's Nazarene church sits somewhere between the two, with a mix of both written and extemporaneous prayers and liturgies, no-frills musical worship, a sermon, and the Eucharist.

Liturgy provides anxious teenagers with comforting routines. As we say and sing the words from our liturgies, they tell us who we are and how we are supposed to live. In doing so, they form our character. In my (Brad's) congregation, our service always begins with someone reciting a welcome based on Micah 6:8. That means every kid and teenager in our church can recite this passage by heart and understands they are called to do justice, love mercy, and walk humbly with God. Similarly, you can borrow a piece of your community's liturgy and say or sing it each week with teenagers to show them who they are as children of God. When you do, you're not only building upon the work of others but also connecting them to a larger Christian community.

Incorporating communion into your time with young people can be another meaningful way to build upon the work of others. A youth pastor from a Korean American ministry explained, "We did a traditional liturgy. Once I got ordained, we did communion every Sunday. I really emphasized the importance of communion, worship, and reverence." If you're not ordained but serve in a community that ties leading communion to ordination, incorporating communion into youth group can give you a great opportunity to collaborate with your pastors, which will also help teenagers form relationships across your church.

Another way to build on the work of others is to incorporate practices like "passing the peace" or marking yourself with the sign of the cross. One urban congregation we visited on the East Coast noticed the power of blessing during a summer program for local children. Each day, a pastor prayed a blessing over the young people gathered. Before long, staff noticed young people were using the same words to bless one another, particularly when they were on one another's "last nerve." Doing so became a practical way for adults and young people to show patience to one another and remind each other how they are called to live as followers of Jesus day in and day out.

Tell Stories from Your Own Life

Just as Jesus told stories to teach his followers, we need to do the same. To cultivate relationships with young people, tell stories from your own life. Vulnerably sharing your experiences (in age-appropriate ways) communicates that you trust young people. One leader in an urban Catholic church explained, "We use a lot of testimony in talking with young people so that they can see how adults experience God. We tell our volunteers that what students want to know is, 'What is your experience of God now, as a worker, as a spouse, as a parent? Where are you continuing to see the Lord speak to you? How are you responding to that?' Those kinds of stories allow young people to see that we did not have a transformative experience once in high school but daily seek to bring the struggles of life to the Lord and respond."

Not only did youth leaders think telling stories fostered relationship but students we spoke with in our research did too. One teenager in a multiethnic Baptist congregation described how their youth group talks about "mature" youth group topics like race. When they do, they "start with something from the Bible, see what people in the Bible did," hear personal stories from adult leaders' lives, and then consider how they can live out their faith in their own context. Hearing youth leaders' personal stories fosters trust, models growth, and helps form their character.

I (Jen) was reminded of how stories foster relationships just the other night, when our youth group was debating whether God exists. A young skeptic said emphatically that faith and science contradict each other. In response, I shared how, as a science-minded teenager, I grew up wondering that too. What convinced me that the two were not incompatible wasn't the Bible. It was working in the high-energy physics department at a national laboratory and meeting doctoral-level scientists who believed in God—not in spite of their career in science but because of it. After I shared that story, another student with whom I'd struggled to connect told me, "I've always wanted to be a scientist, but as a Christian, I didn't think I could. Thanks for showing me otherwise."

Invite Teenagers to Tell Stories

Once you've shared your own story, invite students to tell theirs. In many traditions, this practice of sharing stories is known as *testimony*. Testimonies do not need to follow a certain formula to be powerful. One leader from a multiethnic Catholic ministry cautioned, "A testimony is not necessarily giving you my entire life story in the faith. It's 'We're reading this Scripture passage, and this is how it intersects with my life right now. I'm kind of wrestling with how to live it out.'"

The process of giving a testimony can help young people form their faith and character. Amanda Drury, author of *Saying*

Is Believing, describes how testimonies form "our present and future selves" because those who share their stories are "doing more than describing; they [are] constructing."[13] She elaborates, "When an individual is able to articulate where and how he understands God to be present in his life, this articulation can serve as a kind of legitimating apparatus, and one's description of God's presence in the past may help bolster one's present faith."[14] It may also do the same for the listener, in part by providing them with real-life examples of how faith and character can be practiced beyond youth group.

Given the power of testimony, it is wise to intentionally find ways to incorporate it into your ministry. One youth leader from a Presbyterian congregation requires confirmands—those teenagers publicly affirming through confirmation the promises their parents made for them during infant baptism—to create a statement of faith that says what they believe and why they believe it. In the same congregation, high school seniors are then invited to give testimonies about what God and the church mean to them. Through this practice, young people construct their future selves during two critical milestones in their faith development—confirmation and graduation.

"In our [bilingual Latina/o] church, we have a practice called *convivio*. If you translate the Spanish to English, con is 'with' and vivio is vivir, 'to live.' So it means 'to do life with.' Very early on in the ministry, we decided to have these convivios. It's kind of like a potluck, but people would share their testimony and a little bit about themselves. And that created a lot more room for empathy and for connection within the congregation as we started to grow. And so when we started being more authentic with one another in the youth ministry, it wasn't too unfamiliar for some of my youth to really share."

Tell Stories Together

Besides inviting individuals to tell their stories, you can also create stories together. One youth pastor shared with us how, during the pandemic, their group came to church, talked about what was happening, and explored a Bible story. Then they would reenact, film, and play that story on Zoom on Fridays. According to this leader, "It was a way for everyone to talk about Bible characters like they were real people right now." Creatively retelling the story enabled young people to see that biblical figures are real men and women living out (or sometimes failing to live out) their Christlike character, a process that prepared them to do the same in their own lives.

Ask Questions to Determine What Teenagers Care About

In addition to telling stories, you can also teach for transformation by asking questions like Jesus did. Start by asking teenagers questions to find out what they care about. In our research, leaders regularly told us how important it is to let students' questions and needs drive our teaching. One leader from an Orthodox church suggested, "Part of leadership formation and development is learning to take the time to meet people where they are and address personal and individual needs."

I (Jen) wish I'd understood this sooner in my youth ministry career. Remember the story that opened this chapter? Had I taken the time to ask questions to find out what students in my ministry cared about (and then really listened to their answers), their frustrations might not have escalated to the point of involving my boss. Beyond that, I would have been a better youth leader because I would have helped them integrate their faith into their everyday lives by talking about what mattered most to them.

Use Questions to Explore a Variety of Important Topics

Letting students' questions and needs drive your teaching doesn't mean ignoring important theological topics. It means strategically integrating them into the conversations young people want to have anyway, even if they're about polarizing and controversial topics.

- Talking about climate change opens the door to talk about God's creation and Genesis 1–3.
- Talking about immigration connects naturally to stories of migration throughout Scripture (there are dozens!).
- Talking about gender identity could lead to a connection with the ways gender is addressed in both the Old and New Testaments.

While talking about controversial topics may make you uncomfortable, if you care about the long-term formation of young people's character, ignoring them is not an option. How can teenagers trust us if we refuse to wrestle with the topics they care most about?

The truth is, they can't.

We saw this especially vividly in one ethnically and politically diverse church we visited. As the 2020 national election approached, the church held a public forum about voting, with two of the church's highly respected lay leaders sharing who they were voting for and why. One was voting for the Democratic candidate, and the other was voting for the Republican candidate. When we hosted focus groups at this church a year later, teenagers, small group leaders, parents, and the pastor all mentioned the power of this public forum in letting all generations in the community know that committed Jesus followers could disagree about key issues.

If diving into controversial subjects makes you anxious, approach these topics more like Jesus. Instead of being the answer person, ask questions. Make it clear you don't have all the answers. As one youth leader explained, "The discussion then becomes about, 'Let's really try to understand this ourselves.'"

> If you need additional help addressing the tough questions your teenagers are asking, consider using Jen's Deeper Questions curriculum available at TheYouthCartel.com.
>
> If you'd like to specifically address race, culture, and immigration with young people, see FYI's "Talking about Race with Teenagers" guide and the Who Do You Say I Am? curriculum, both available at FullerYouthInstitute .org.

Ask Questions to Teach

Once you learn what young people care about and begin addressing difficult topics, teach by asking questions.

That's right. Stop only giving talks. Instead, create question-based discussions.

If the thought of teaching by asking questions fills you with fear and trepidation like it did me (Jen) when it became clear that's what my students longed for, remember that asking questions is not shirking your duties as a teacher. It *is* possible to actually teach young people and form their faith and character by asking questions. (Again, that's what Jesus did!)

To teach by asking questions, decide what point you would like to make and then write a series of questions that enable young people to reach that destination one step at a time.

As you lead question-based discussions, occasionally play devil's advocate. When everyone in the room agrees, argue the other side. Challenge teenagers to think deeply about an issue so they can find their voice, understand what they believe and why, and become "ethical thinkers" inside and outside youth group.[15]

Use Ground Rules to Create Safety for Teenagers to Ask and Answer Questions

To ensure everyone's voice is valued during question-based teaching, establish ground rules. These can be as simple as stating, "Every voice matters. Only one person speaks at a time. Listen to each person's full idea. Ask questions to clarify what someone said. Feel free to disagree, but do so respectfully."

Alternatively, you can cocreate covenants with your group to foster the safety needed for young people to ask and answer questions. One multiracial Episcopal youth group collectively wrote a "Rule of Life" that says, "We pray together, we eat together, and we love, care, and listen for each other." This rule of life helps teenagers understand how they will relate to one another when they are gathered. When they recite these words together, they remind one another what kind of people they are, an act that is critical in building trust and forming character.

When a teenager says something you fear the senior pastor would say is heresy, utilize these four strategies to course-correct without shaming:

Pull out a nugget of truth from whatever the teenager said. Rather than correct everything, acknowledge what was right and build on that.

Ask, "What does everyone else think?" to give young people and other adult leaders the opportunity to offer different (and often more orthodox!) viewpoints. When you do this, you can even explicitly call on a student or adult you trust to answer the question correctly.

Answer the question yourself, but do so conversationally, as another person sharing their opinion.

Share your church's position on whatever you're talking about.

Tips for Utilizing Question-Based Teaching in Large Contexts

If you lead a bigger ministry, you probably recognize you cannot lead one question-based conversation with hundreds of teenagers (or maybe even dozens of them). You can, however, find creative ways to share the mic, just like leaders in our research did.

- Host panel discussions so diverse people can share stories from their own lives and relate them to Bible topics. Then give students a chance to ask the panelists questions after they share.
- Talk for shorter time periods and interject questions into your talks. Have people share their responses to your questions in pairs or small groups, and then ask a few to explain their thinking with the big group. Then build upon what they are saying. Elevate the voices of others by drawing out the good in what has been said and tying it to the point you are trying to make.
- Prioritize small groups. Small groups give everyone the chance to speak and be heard.

Commission Others and Share Your Authority

Just as Jesus commissioned his followers and shared his authority with them, if we want to teach for transformation, we need to commission teens for ministry. To understand what type of ministry to commission teenagers for, intentionally explore spiritual gifts together. One leader in a predominantly White setting described the importance of this by saying, "We want kids to understand at a very practical level that God has given them a unique ability to minister. If they don't do it, then it may not get done."

Spiritual gifts assessments or tools (like the APEST inventory developed by missiologist Alan Hirsch) can also be useful in helping teenagers discover their gifts. Knowing teenagers' gifts helps you put them on the "right seat on the bus"[16] so they can serve and lead well.

As you explore various gifts with young people, practice affirmation. At the end of retreats, camps, or mission trips, call out the character traits you have seen in one another. One pastor told us how she takes time at the end of camp "to express how they've grown, however small that may be, and to be encouraged by the body [of Christ]." Affirmation times like these become "life incubators" for teenagers that allow them to leave your time together committed to living out their Christlike character in the real world. This affirmation may be especially catalytic in students' lives because you may be the first adult—either in a long time or ever—who names how well particular young people are living out Jesus' goodness by loving their neighbors.

Let Teenagers Lead

Another way to help young people discover their gifts (and purpose!) is to let them lead. Some leaders we interviewed leaned more into student leadership during the pandemic out of necessity. One frustrated leader explained how students' lack of engagement in their church's online worship prompted them to invite teenagers to lead worship themselves from their homes via Instagram Lives. When students led, their peers' engagement increased.

You can also proactively ask young people to serve as small group or worship leaders, even if they aren't ready to be "solo" leaders in either context. In fact, partnering teens with adults in leadership is ideal.

My (Kara's) young adult son, Nathan, recently visited us and joined us for worship. Unlike most weekend worship services, there was no lead vocalist; the worship team took turns leading particular choruses throughout the service. Afterward, Nathan specifically noted that he liked how the worship leadership was shared among team members, especially since it was a group that was diverse in gender, age, and ethnicity.

Equip Teenagers to Teach

Additionally, share your authority with young people by asking them not only to lead but also to teach. As you might recall from the story that began this chapter, my (Jen's) students desperately wanted to teach their peers. Because I wanted to keep my job, I reluctantly created a process for this.

First, teenagers chose the topics, which meant that from my vantage point as an adult, we explored some strange issues. Often we'd alternate who chose, so while one week we'd talk about how justice demands we consider our purchasing power, the next we'd talk about whether dead pets went to heaven. A week focused on the injustice of war would be followed by a conversation about whether God created aliens.

After choosing their topic, teenagers would research it (I would give them good, theologically robust resources), find ways to integrate the Bible into the conversation, and then submit a draft of their lesson to me. We would then explore their lesson together and, where appropriate, insert doctrine into the conversation. Because teenagers cared deeply about their chosen topic, they worked hard to prepare their lesson, often investigating Scripture in ways they seldom did on their own.

A youth leader we interviewed from a Latina/o Southern Baptist congregation observed this too. When a student of his began leading Sunday school, she would "study the Bible beyond what was asked of her." This led to her "tremendous growth."

Not only do teenagers grow in their faith when they teach but their friends often do too. When teenagers teach, their friends support them. They participate in discussions differently, with greater attention and more thoughtful comments. Often friends stick around, intrigued by a church where their peers occasionally lead tricky conversations.

Create Student Leadership Teams to Share Your Authority

Another way to both form character and share your authority with young people is to create formal student leadership teams. According to one youth leader from a Reformed congregation, "One of my very first students on the leadership team was a girl who hated me because I was new. One day, I called her into leadership. I shared that I saw more in her and that if she was interested in leading, I was interested in teaching and training her how. That changed her world."

As this leader can attest, student leadership forms (and transforms) young people. Once again, in this leader's words, "I take that kind of rough student. If they have leadership ability, I take them onto this team. They help set direction and vision.

I personally pour more attention into that group. One-on-one discipleship happens there."

As student leaders face various leadership challenges, they exhibit and refine their character. The more they do, the more they catch character and live it out beyond youth group.

As we mentioned in chapter 5, FYI's research for our book *Growing Young* found that churches engaging young people well invest in what we call "keychain leadership," giving keys of access and authority to young people so they can serve in significant and meaningful ways in ministry of all kinds. See FullerYouthInstitute.org to learn more about *Growing Young* and our training and assessment services for your church.

Mel's Transformation

Mel's family started attending my (Jen's) church just before her freshman year. Because of the influence of the students who wanted more and better discussions, by the time Mel's family joined our church, I taught by asking questions rather than lecturing. As Mel participated in these discussions, our entire group quickly learned who Mel was. Her gift of compassion and heart for justice were evident. A decade later, she recalls, "I knew I found my place when you asked some spicy question in a discussion. It was the first time I heard people talk about questions and doubts in church."

Before long, Mel got involved as our community welcomed refugees. She built on the work of others, learning from older high schoolers—like Ryan, whom we met in chapter 1—how to welcome refugees. After countless visits to welcome reset-tled families from around the globe into our neighborhood, Mel suggested our youth ministry could become equipped to welcome people at a moment's notice by stocking our closet with the most needed supplies. We commissioned Mel to lead that collection process among our entire congregation.

The more Mel welcomed refugees, the more her empathy and compassion increased. Filled with a sense of purpose, she brought their stories—which became part of her story—back to our community and shared them as she led discussions about the "refugee highway," the path refugees take to move from the country they're fleeing to the one in which they're resettling.

Today, Mel works full-time for an agency that resettles refugees. The character that was formed through transformational teaching in our ministry is still evident every time she picks up a displaced family from the airport and works with volunteers to compassionately resettle them in a way that dignifies and honors their humanity.

While Mel never met the student leaders who'd forced me to rethink my teaching years beforehand, her life and faith were dramatically shaped by them. When we teach for transformation, the ripples of faith beyond youth group extend further than we could ever imagine.

REFLECTION QUESTIONS

1. Think about how you currently teach. Do your teaching methods equip young people to live out a character-filled faith beyond youth group? If so, how?

2. What is your mental model (or "picture in your head") for youth ministry teaching, and what most influenced it?

3. Review the barriers to teaching for transformation: our mental models, our misplaced focus, and Gen Z's

distrust of authority. Which do you struggle with most in your context?

4. How does your ministry utilize storytelling? Whose stories do you need to hear more of?

5. What issues and topics do young people in your ministry care most about? How do you know? How regularly do you teach on these topics?

6. What might you gain by utilizing more questions (and fewer talks) to teach young people? What might you lose? How might such a shift contribute to teenagers' faith development?

7. Who is a teenager in your ministry you would like to see teach? How could you equip them to teach in your ministry?

SEVEN

PRACTICE TOGETHER

Character That Moves through Teenagers' Hands and Feet

Contributing Author: Yulee Lee

Yulee Lee served as senior director of staff culture and diversity, equity, and inclusion at FYI during the last two years of this research project and collaborated on the development of the Faith Beyond Youth Group Compass. Originally from South Korea, Yulee grew up in Salt Lake City and now lives in Chicago. She holds degrees from Tufts University, the University of Chicago, and Trinity Evangelical Divinity School and now serves as the COO of Stuff You Can Use.

"We tried to develop character in teenagers by encouraging them to read the Bible or memorize Scripture," Julian said. "But that often became mechanical, and I didn't feel like character actually mattered to some of the kids."

A White leader at an evangelical church in the southeastern US, Julian wanted to reorient his ministry from going through the motions to living out faith in the world. But how? He and his students were stagnant—and stuck.

So they started trying some new approaches. Julian shared, "We started doing service in the community to give them more hands-on practical stuff, working with people, working with children and kids. We started going to a free health clinic here in town and got the kids involved in washing feet. Of course, you can imagine not everybody likes to do that. We would do some other things like go to an Alzheimer's unit and hang out with people and feed them and make cards. Doing these kinds of things seemed to be a better teacher than just having students read or study."

Just like with this notable youth group, countless stories in our research showed that *practice moves us beyond the head and heart; it takes us into our bodies.* We live, try, and experiment with what it means to love God and others at home, at school, and in everyday situations.

My (Yulee's) church's youth group organized a simpler yet equally powerful time of practicing together by partnering with a local school to create spaces of beauty and belonging for their increasingly international student population, who miss the aesthetics of their home countries.

Similar to logging driving hours with an adult before getting an official driver's license, young people need practice in responding with character to the many crossroads in their life journeys. That's why *practice together* is the next point in our Faith Beyond Youth Group Compass.

The cycle of practice (action) and making meaning (reflection) is an important part of adolescents' character and identity formation process. This chapter will zero in on the practice of character, and chapter 8 will focus on helping young people make sense of their actions and experiences.

Cultivating Christlike character through this action-reflection cycle is a journey best taken in the context of community—and youth groups can be greenhouses of character growth. Being seen makes it possible for young people to know their identity in Christ and discover God's purpose for their lives as they practice loving God and others in the real world—together *with* you.

According to youth ministry scholar Andrew Root,

> [Ministry] is not about "using" relationships to get individuals to accept a "third thing," whether that be conservative politics, moral behaviors or even the gospel message. Rather, ministry is about connection, one to another, about sharing in suffering and joy, about persons meeting persons with no pretense or secret motives. It is about shared life, confessing Christ not outside the relationship but within it. This, I learned, was living the gospel.[1]

Living the gospel involves practicing the gospel. Character-forming practices are the repeated, communal actions that form faith beyond youth group in the everyday lives of young people. Think of each day as a chain of experiments in character formation. Young people are sent out to test the virtues they've learned in relationships through modeling and teaching in the church and youth ministry.

We give young people the space and opportunity to practice their faith and character, fail, receive grace, and try again. In the struggles of everyday life, they develop character competence and, eventually, begin to own their faith.

Why Practicing Together Matters

Practicing Together Helps Students "See, Do, Teach"

"See, do, teach" is the learning process that Dr. Steve Lee, my (Yulee's) senior pastor, went through at the teaching hospital where he trained as a medical doctor. (You might have seen this process in one of the medical dramas on TV!) He likens these years of medical training to "being thrown off the ship" with only two choices in front of him: sink or swim.

This learning process would entail first watching (see) a more experienced doctor conduct a procedure, often only once. Then, Steve would conduct (do) the same procedure himself on the next patient who needed it while the more experienced doctors guided him. It was during this "do" part of the process Steve prayed that his doing, which in fact was like practicing, would not result in deadly outcomes. With each successful procedure, Steve realized that practicing his skills, regardless of how messy it felt, was the only way to become a competent doctor. Only after practicing enough could Steve "teach" others himself.

Practicing who God means for us to be helps us engage our whole bodies, minds, and souls to grow more spiritually healthy and mature. Christian practices researcher Dorothy Bass captures this when she writes,

> With practice, you also become a more welcoming person, a better friend, a stronger advocate for justice, and a more caring part of creation—not all at once, perhaps, and never perfectly. But through practice, you become a little more involved in the loving, challenging life of God.[2]

Practicing Together Builds Muscle Memory

One ministry in our research painted a great picture of why practicing together matters to young people's ability to put on Christlike character in situations outside the ministry. "We encourage young people and adults alike to do the unglamorous service. The cleaning that nobody is going to see or notice or give you praise for. We encourage them to look for how God shows up when they are stepping into an unknown, potentially scary situation," we were told. "As a participant in our ministry, you will not know what is going to happen when we serve our neighbors together, but every single time you will encounter Christ in the people you are serving with as well as in the people you are serving. Once young people serve others in these ways, it becomes easier, for example, to have compassion on people in your own family. Service through our ministry creates muscle memory that leads to service in their homes."

Examples like this can help us prioritize practicing together because we can tangibly see how it creates "muscle memory" for teenagers to draw from as they live out their faith beyond youth group.

Practicing Together Equips You as a Discipler of Teenagers

Leaders who practice character in their own lives are better equipped to instill it in the lives of young people. In chapter 5 we introduced Pastor Christina from Forest Hills Covenant Church in Boston. She connected modeling with practicing together: "I try to practice a number of things, such as activism, but also things like using reusable dishes at youth group. What I've learned from practicing helps me practice better together with young people, like writing letters to government officials or going with one of my teens to a Black Lives Matter protest after George Floyd was murdered."

Just like this youth leader, when we practice an everyday faith, we influence a community of generosity through who we are to each other and the world. We learn more of who God desires us to be. Practicing together is a gift that keeps on giving. When we practice character, we can give character. As we give character, we receive character. In this relationally tethered rhythm, discipleship becomes a gift rather than a guilt trip.

Practicing Together Engages Teenagers' Whole Bodies

Practicing together matters because, as we discussed in chapter 6, character development is not just about head knowledge. It's a holistic engagement of our heart, soul, mind, and strength.

This makes sense because we are not just thinking beings; we are also physical and emotional beings. Research shows that no matter who we are, our initial physiological response to a stimulus is embodied and emotional.[3] This reality is even more pronounced for teens who have experienced trauma and whose bodies "keep score" of those events and their accompanying emotions like fear, shame, and anger.[4]

Although the degree of trauma is different for each teenager and is influenced by factors such as social location, systemic racism, and other intersectional[5] realities, *all* young people have experienced collective trauma throughout the COVID-19 pandemic.

This generation is more attuned than most adults to approaching life holistically. Mindfulness, wellness, and self-care practices are part of their lexicon. By engaging teenagers' whole bodies in the process of character formation and by reinforcing that our whole bodies matter to God, we can catalyze the collective healing we all need.

Practicing Together Elevates Others over Ourselves

By creating character-forming communities of practice, we champion inclusion by elevating others over ourselves. James K. A. Smith makes a similar point when he states:

> Formative youth ministry eschews entertainment for service. The sorts of activities that keep young people entertained are often highly relative to cultural, socioeconomic, and even racial preferences. What sounds like "fun" to one group will be alienating for another; or the sorts of experiences expected by one group might be fiscally out of reach for another.[6]

By contrast, he writes, "service to others can have a kind of leveling effect."[7] In other words, practicing together reorients our focus toward others through our joint calling to love our neighbors.

Practicing together can increase our time with young people by engaging them in opportunities outside regular youth group to love God and others through protesting, serving in food pantries, participating in mission trips, and more. When young people are invited into Jesus-centered, character-forming communities of practice like these, our ministry hours with young people multiply along with our shared faith!

Ultimately, character will matter for young people if they can see why it matters for the world. Practicing together helps us show them why.

Three Barriers to Practicing Together

While practicing together is important, it's not easy. In fact, youth leaders and teenagers each face specific barriers to life-giving activities that can build both character and faith beyond youth group.

1. Leaders Lack Wisdom

First, youth leaders may not have much wisdom from lived experience themselves. While today's youth leaders span generations, youth workers still trend young. Full of energy and ideas, and in proximity to teenagers' life stage, young adults may lack familiarity with any number of formative life experiences. And depending on their situation growing up, they may not have experienced much hardship. While young leaders can certainly be effective, this lack of suffering can sometimes be a barrier. In contrast, leaders who have lived through character-shaping trials offer unique wisdom to young people undergoing similar experiences.

For example, our research found that leaders who were most equipped to help shape the character of young people who experience suffering were leaders who wrestled with suffering themselves—and also had developed a working theology of suffering. In the words of one leader: "Internal peace is something we should pursue because external circumstances can be disturbed at any time. So I think perseverance looks like remaining in my calling to be a good and faithful servant through any circumstance. I don't have a lot of 'It's okay! You can do it!' in me. Those responses almost dismiss my actual struggles. The same thing happens when people just say to young people, 'Keep going! You'll be okay!' Sometimes you won't be okay. I will say that a lot to teenagers. Based on my own life experiences, sometimes things are not going to be okay the way you think okay looks. But if we actually have trust and hope that *God is okay*, we'll show up and *we'll be okay* because he is there."

In this way, wounded healers often become the best ministers to young people.[8] Similar sentiments were shared by one leader in a Latina/o church community: "What perseverance looked like for me in my testimony was not going to look the same in a teenager's testimony, and what perseverance looked like for their parents was not going to look the same for them. So, the way we share about perseverance is through our own experiences and through our own lives, but without having an agenda of what it was going to look like for them at the end because that was for them to explore. These conversations get really messy because teenagers are used to just getting answers for everything, and we often feel the expectation of having all the answers."

2. Opportunities Are Out of Reach

Second, our opportunities may seem out of reach to young people. Teenagers are busier than ever, which limits their time within our ministry to practice together. Many young people also lack the financial means and relational support necessary to practice together in the ways we plan.

Some teenagers belong to families who feel like the kinds of "practice" we're talking about can be risky and maybe even a departure from how they handle things as a family unit. *What if my teenager is exposed to people who are dangerous? When will my kid learn about God if they're protesting in the streets?* These might be some of the questions running through the minds of well-intentioned and loving parents and guardians who want their teenagers to love and follow God all the days of their lives.

A lack of finances can also hinder a young person's ability to practice together. In most churches we know, international mission trips often come with a price tag that prohibits, or at least discourages, some teenagers from even trying to raise funds. It's not only international trips but also camps and retreats that exceed families' household budget capacity. One youth leader pointed out, "My ministry is very limited in a lot of cases. Probably 75–80 percent of our families are first-generation immigrants. This means they have to give up a lot. Many of our teens can't afford to go on retreats. Mom and Dad have to work two or three shifts just to make ends meet."

3. It's Complicated

Third, social location complicates virtue development. For some teenagers, the qualities required to live and love like Jesus every day are developed through life circumstances beyond their control as well as through their social location (gender, race, ethnicity, socioeconomic status, abilities, and other social identity markers). Our research shows that humility and forgiveness, for example, appear to be difficult virtues to develop in certain clusters of young people.

The lived experiences of immigrants and minorities can make it difficult for their leaders to focus on humility in particular. In the words of one church leader serving in an immigrant church: "There is a difference between being humiliated and living humbly. Some of the parents have had to live in the shadows because they're undocumented. There's this automatic sense to not center oneself. But there are also some parents who've been trampled over and actually humiliated. Yes, to humble yourself is to lower yourself in some way and not put your importance above another's. But I think that's something the parents already experience, and that does affect the way the students see themselves."

Another church leader serving typically marginalized youth explained, "Our young people have to fight every day to prove themselves and to receive respect and love from society. When all they know about themselves through experience is to be put down, the natural reaction is contrary to that—fighting, gasping for air. So [they say,] 'Don't tell me about humility, because society has been putting me down for so long. Don't tell me about forgiveness.' Not because young people don't want to forgive, because I know that the hope is there. But because there have been a lot of wounds and young people are still not healed. And they are too raw to heal from these wounds."

Affluence also presents complications in forming humility in young people. According to one leader serving in a higher income community, "That you are loved, you are enough are messages I drill into them, hoping that head knowledge turns into heart knowledge, but I think [their affluence] blinds them from some humility."

Developing forgiveness in young people is also challenging in particular cultures. For example, young people may harbor ill-will toward parents for how they "do things," when in fact the way they "do things" may be cultural in nature. Many Asian cultures also value pride and loyalty, two traits that often make forgiving others particularly difficult. Likewise, there are hints in our research that forgiveness may be tied to perseverance because of the ways in which minoritized communities disproportionately experience injustice. Often these communities learn to carry on without focusing too much on forgiving because there are other more pressing practical matters. These communities also know from personal experience how much forgiveness is often about more than two individuals. It's also about systems and generational trauma.

Character development involves taking into account painful realities and the need to change the systems that create those realities while not dehumanizing or villainizing the people who have been resisting oppression. It also takes into account that for some harms, true forgiveness can take years—regardless of cultural background or social location. Young people should not be rushed by our ideals.

How Jesus Practiced Together

"God doesn't require anything of us except to receive this love that will change everything. This will guide what we do, not be a list of requirements.... God's invitation, then, is to be radiant in reflecting God's own tenderness in the world." —Father Gregory Boyle[9]

Receiving God's love shapes our identity and motivations for practice. Being love himself, Jesus is the prime example of what it looks like to practice together as an act of worship and witness in the world.

What we *don't* want to do is communicate an idealized Christianity to young people by overfocusing on Jesus' perfect example and shaming or pressuring them into behavior modification. Rather, we want to communicate that throughout the disbelief, mistakes, and failures of his disciples, *Jesus never abandoned them*. He showed up again and again to practice together and live out the kingdom of God every day. As a result, Jesus and his disciples journeyed together toward healing and wholeness.

Thankfully, Jesus shows us in his own practice with the disciples that building character takes time, multiple tries, and at least two people.

Practicing in Twos

Calling the Twelve to him, he began to send them out two by two and gave them authority over impure spirits.

These were his instructions: "Take nothing for the journey except a staff—no bread, no bag, no money in your belts. Wear sandals but not an extra shirt." (Mark 6:7–9)

Before we reach these verses in Mark 6, Jesus teaches, trains, and disciples his followers how to live out kingdom principles. The disciples have a front-row seat to Jesus' preaching on the kingdom of God. They see miraculous healings take place. They watch Jesus interact with people from all sorts of places and positions.

Jesus then sends his disciples to practice the same things he did: preaching, healing the sick, and freeing people from demonic possession. Jesus knows they can't do it alone. Instead, they need to practice together with their trusted friends and ministry partners. Even as they go, Jesus tells his disciples to take nothing with them; as they work together, they can depend on Jesus and trust him to be present in their practice.

For young people today, belonging and purpose go hand in hand, and they are activated when we practice together—with even just one other believer.

Practicing Multiple Times over Time

As dedicated as the disciples are, it's no secret they make big mistakes. Jesus is okay with that. He gives them opportunities to practice, fail, and practice again. Jesus never forsakes them, despite their obvious flaws and inadequacies. He always comes back the next day to practice together again.

The apostle John experienced the unfailing love of Jesus in the midst of his failures. In Luke 9:54, James and John discover that a Samaritan village won't receive Jesus. They respond by asking, "Lord, do You want us to command fire to come down from heaven and consume them?" (NASB). Perhaps due to underdeveloped emotional agility, James and John think the best response is to sacrifice the lives of the villagers in order to advance the gospel. (If you don't remember what happened next, I'll leave that cliff-hanger for you to resolve!)

Much later, after more people in Samaria have responded to the gospel (Acts 8:14), Peter and John are commissioned to help them receive the Holy Spirit. From this progression, we see that not only was Jesus patient with John when John was rash but he also gave John authority to keep practicing, and, ultimately, to share the gift of the Spirit with people he had wanted to destroy.

Just like the disciples, today's anxious, adaptive, and diverse young people looking for purpose are asking the question "What difference can I make in the world?" When young people practice together with their community of faith, they can better understand an answer not only to that question but also to their parallel questions of identity and belonging.

Navigational Tools for Practicing Together

Practicing together can feel time-consuming and even expensive, but we can break through those barriers with some creativity. Through our team's site visits, research, and our own experiences, we've assembled some navigational tools you can try, along with stories of what they look like in real youth ministries.

Practice Together through Addressing Current Events

During my (Yulee's) site visit to a multiethnic ministry in Chicago, their youth gathering was focused on compassion, with the youth leader first talking about what compassion looked like in her own life. She then asked, "How can we show compassion and love others who are far away from us?"

Through this question, she engaged young people in a reflection about the fifty-three migrants who had recently died after being trapped in a tractor trailer in Texas. They dialogued together about how they could pray for that situation, and how the young people could be God's agents of change so these kinds of deaths might be prevented in the future. Then they took ten minutes to compassionately pray together.

Here's a road map for how (often tragic) current events like this one can be a springboard for you to practice character with the teenagers in your community:

- Highlight a current event.
- Share how the event influenced you.
- Invite students to share their own thoughts and feelings about the event.
- Ask students to read relevant Scripture passages.
- Invite students into a time of lament.[10]
- Identify resources and brainstorm practical steps your ministry can take to help.
- Commit to practicing together in the next several months.
- Pray together.
- Revisit your commitments in a week or two to reflect and to adjust anything that should be changed.

Practice Together by Empowering Students to Lead

Just as we looked at ways students can lead through teaching in chapter 6, it's important to name ways students can lead when it comes to practicing together.

Another church in our research reimagined their ministry philosophy and now operates from the belief that youth ministry is youth *doing* ministry. As an example of the impact of this switch, the youth leader shared, "One of our student leaders helps lead the worship team on Wednesday nights, which is completely student led. When we say we believe youth ministry is youth doing ministry, our whole model and mindset is that we don't want to just teach young people how to do church; we want to teach young people to do *life*. So not only has she grown in her faith and basic devotion and disciplines, but I've also seen her leadership develop and character start to blossom."

Here's a road map from my (Yulee's) own church for how you can practice this together with the teenagers in your community:

- *Identify the values you want your youth ministry to be known for.* One of our values is inclusion, so we decided to emphasize love and belonging in the rest of this process.

- *Conduct a listening session with young people to learn how they experience belonging in your ministry.* In our listening sessions, we learned that one teenager felt included when he was invited to drum on the praise team while another felt belonging while serving in the children's ministry.

- *Invite young people to practice loving others* through service opportunities that align with your ministry values *and* align with young people's experience of those values. So with the examples above, we invited the drummer to join our praise team more regularly, and we invited the other teenager to serve consistently alongside our children's pastor.
- *Invite young people to lead when the time is right.* After he had served for several months on the praise team, we invited the drummer to put together worship sets for family services and to communicate plans to the worship team. Today, this teenager leads the praise team on his own, making beautiful mistakes along the way!
- *Connect with young people to help them process what they're learning and how they're growing in Christlike character.* Once a month, we invite these student leaders to a leadership team meeting where our youth pastor leads them in a devotional and helps them connect their service to who they're becoming in Christ.

Practice Together by Holistically Engaging Teenagers

Given that trauma impacts so many young people, holistic ministry can engage students' whole beings. Specifically, body-centered practices such as paced breathing, mindful meditation, and prayer walks can help trauma survivors feel safe to experience traumatic grief without feeling overwhelmed. These types of practices help survivors connect to the compassion and goodness of God, which opens the portal to exploring compassion and goodness in themselves and others.[11]

Along these lines, one youth leader in our research shared about the importance of practicing together through "trauma-informed discipleship" (a ministry approach in which leaders give consideration to the needs of teens who have endured hard circumstances). To do this, she designed a consistent rhythm for teenagers to engage—some together and some on their own: Sunday morning worship, Monday Bible study, Thursday spiritual formation with prayer practices, and Saturday outreach activities.

For example, on a Sunday, they might talk about the suffering in the world and how God is calling young people to address it. Then on Monday, their Bible study explores what healing can look like. Thursday is for body-focused practices such as breath work, contemplative prayer, engaging the outdoors, or mindful eating. This is to help teenagers understand that "you can't think your way out of" trauma. Finally, Saturday is a day to practice on their own and with neighbors and friends.

Another leader shared about their healing prayer ministry in response to young people's trauma. "We teach a lot about forgiveness and allowing God to work through our woundedness. We say that forgiving something is not forgetting it or saying that injustice did not happen, or that it was okay that somebody would hurt us, or it was okay that we chose to hurt someone. But instead, [we're] saying that we don't have to let all that become toxic to us; we can give ourselves space to heal. Even if we have to end a relationship, we can say, 'I wish' and 'I hope' that person could be well, or could get healing, or could face justice in a merciful way, without me needing revenge or anything beyond having the space to heal myself."

Become Equipped to Provide Trauma-Informed Care

You may want to explore more resources for you and your team to better serve young people who have experienced trauma of various kinds, including a range of adverse childhood experiences (ACEs) such as abuse, neglect, or community violence, which can cumulatively impact young people's well-being. Research shows that over one-quarter of Gen Zers report experiencing four or more ACEs, the most of any current generation.[12] Here are a few resources to get started:

» Trauma Healing Institute: TraumaHealingInstitute.org/About

» *SCARS: Trauma Informed Discipleship* video-based training for leaders by Urban Youth Workers Institute: UYWI.org

» *The FYI on Youth Ministry Podcast* episode on trauma informed discipleship with psychologist David Wang: FullerYouthInstitute.org/Podcast (or wherever you listen to podcasts)

» Child Mind Institute's resources on trauma and grief: ChildMind.org

» Echo trauma and resilience training for families, leaders, and organizations: EchoTraining.org

Practice Hospitality Together to Welcome Outsiders

Consider how you welcome new young people into your ministry. Your faith community likely already has a process for welcoming outsiders to become insiders—of demonstrating hospitality. Just as your larger community might collect information from new families, you can ask teenagers to fill out information cards so you can connect with them outside youth group. Like churches who connect older members with newer folks, you can pair up veteran students with newbies to ensure everyone is known and cared for. If your congregation has a ritual for joining the church, you can also create rituals that help you welcome newcomers to your youth ministry.

You can also proactively build bridges to help students transition from one life stage ministry to another. One youth pastor in a large multicampus church identified a time of limbo between the end of sixth grade and the start of seventh, which coincided with the beginning of their middle school ministry. After listening to sixth graders express their fears about moving into the youth ministry, this pastor intentionally hosted a class to address their fears by showing them what they'd encounter in youth group.

Another way to practice hospitality is by meeting kids on their turf rather than expecting them to come to church. Just as care teams take food to families celebrating the birth of a baby or mourning the death of a loved one, you can also drop off goodie bags at young people's homes during strategic moments of the year, like when teens are particularly stressed as they start a new school year or prepare for finals.

When young people feel like their whole selves are welcome in our ministries, they will likely want other newcomers to feel welcome too.

Practice Together to Make What's Novel Normal

"I'm thinking particularly about the effect that YES has had on my life, and my family's life as well. I've been going on YES trips since I was in eighth grade and then became a junior leader and now lead trips fully. I've been able to bring back all of my stories to my family. Sometimes they're stories about people we have met, or served, and conversations we've had with those people. Sometimes they are conversations or stories about the participants on the trip. And it's been really cool to watch my parents' perspectives on homelessness change throughout the years.

"There was one trip when my parents volunteered to help out. They got to serve at an organization that serves meals and provides clothing. My dad felt really connected to the ministry and connected to all of the stories that I had brought home, so he started serving breakfast at a local ministry on Fridays before work, just as part of his life. He got to know a group of men there and became their friend, really. Even when the pandemic shut down that service for a while, my dad would still go get pizzas once a month and hang out in the park with his friends. It's been cool to watch how my dad spends his time serving members of his community and really participating in these peoples' lives, all because of the stories I was able to bring home from my experience through YES."

This young adult shared during one of our research site visits to Youth Equipped to Serve (YES), an organization within the Orthodox Church in North America that works to provide immersive service experiences to congregations and youth groups. The YES team is very intentional about how they create the experience for participants. They focus on doing so in a way that helps students bring what they experience into other parts of their lives—to take what's novel and make it normal.

We've compiled a list of key insights from how they design their experiences to help you better design yours:

- Make sure leaders always participate.
- Serve people's physical needs, but more importantly, look people in the eye and interact with them as image bearers of Christ.

163

- Differentiate between helping and serving by teaching young people that "helping" is when someone of means gives to someone in need, whereas "serving" elevates the other.
- Discourage "I" language (I'm hungry, I'm thirsty, and so on) while serving, because thinking about yourself prevents considering others.
- Do a prayer tour on Friday night before you serve on Saturday. Visit significant areas of the town or city, share information about specific struggles or conditions the people might be facing (like food deserts or locations of trafficking), and have students pray as they feel led.
- Always debrief in a circle. If you're the leader, sit with the participants to be one of them.
- Never ask what students liked or didn't like, because serving isn't about preference. Instead, ask follow-up questions to help students understand why they were feeling what they were feeling.

YES program director Katrina Bitar told us that everything they do in their service work is about "translating the experience into who you are as a human being—becoming someone who doesn't turn their service heart off." This starts with changing the mentality that service is a "project" into one of service as "who we are at our core. We become living sacrifices for others." Their point-in-time work always ends with the question "Now what?" She went on to share, "True service is letting go of your preferences in that moment and saying, 'This is the need in front of me, this is what I'm encountering.'"

Practicing together is messy and somewhat unpredictable. However, there is something powerful about learning through what's happening in the moment. Mistakes and failure are part of the process, so we encourage you to start from where you are, who you are, and with the resources you currently have. Along with your students, you can experience how God can use practicing together to transform both you and your young people.

REFLECTION QUESTIONS

1. Practicing our faith helps young people develop character in real time. How does this insight influence you to think differently about the scope and sequence of your youth ministry?

2. Of the five transformational reasons why practicing matters in youth ministry, which makes the most sense to focus on in your context?

3. How do you think practicing together with their community of faith helps young people better understand Jesus-centered purpose, experience belonging, and holistically embrace who they are in Christ?

4. Which of the barriers to practicing together—leaders lack wisdom, opportunities are out of reach, or complicated dynamics—ring true for you and the young people in your ministry? What ideas do you have for addressing one or more of those barriers?

5. How could you utilize current events to practice character together in your ministry?

6. In what ways are you leveraging student leadership to foster young people's growth?

7. What holistic or trauma-informed navigational tools might you want to try in your youth ministry?

EIGHT

MAKE MEANING

From "What Happened?" to "What Now?"

"We tell our students that if we're waiting fifty-one weeks just to go on this one-week mission trip, we have it backward."

This veteran youth pastor was animated as he explained to our team's interviewer the way their ministry hoped to shift the typical "mission trip" paradigm. Instead of emphasizing a one-week experience serving others in Jesus' name only to return to life as usual, their approach is different. "You go on that one-week mission trip to prepare for the other fifty-one weeks—to determine *who you're going to be* for the other fifty-one weeks."

Whether this Tennessee youth ministry's trips are local, in-state, or out of the country, they always include time to debrief and ask, "What is your fifty-one-week takeaway?" They encourage students to consider something they've learned about themselves or others through the short experience that might change how they relate to others, serve, and live the rest of the year. The leader went on to give some examples. "One student shared, 'I learned the importance of finding those kids nobody is sitting with and really trying to be friends with them. I saw the difference that made. I realized that when I go back to school, I'm going to try to do that for fifty-one other weeks.'

"Another student summarized, 'Well, you know, I learned more about gratitude.' So we asked, 'How can you make gratitude part of your daily identity for fifty-one weeks?'"

This youth ministry is making meaning with students. By *making meaning*, we mean leaders are intentionally reflecting with teenagers on their actions and experiences to spark insight and growth, helping them understand more deeply who they are and who they can be in Jesus. This last compass point is critical to nurture character-forming discipleship and, ultimately, faith beyond youth group.

We all want young people to find their fifty-one-week takeaway, don't we? When we create environments where teenagers can reflect on their experiences, we help them. In the midst of once-a-year and week-to-week experiences, teenagers wonder, *What happened? What does it mean? Where is God? What now?*

Faithful leaders guide students through cycles of action and reflection, tapping into the power of naming experiences, evaluating actions, and connecting to the larger biblical narrative before they go out and try again.

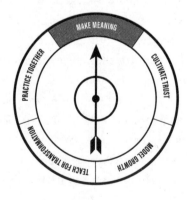

Why Making Meaning Makes a Difference

> "Life can only be understood backwards; but it must be lived forwards."
> —Søren Kierkegaard.[1]

Meaning-makers shape how we see the world. Kierkegaard, Martin Luther King Jr., C. S. Lewis, Toni Morrison, and Mahatma Gandhi were influential primarily because they helped people make meaning in profoundly unsettling times. Or think of Oprah Winfrey's power to shape conversations and draw in an audience, or why so many viewers tune in to hear late-night comedians' clever twists on the week's news. *Interpretation is everything.*

Good interpreters appeal to teenagers too. Taylor Swift's creative genius is at least in part a reflection of her ability to make meaning through her lyrics of lost relationships, new relationships, and peculiar details that tap into universal longings.

Poets, artists, and musicians all take us beyond the realms of reason and logic. And this is what pastoral leaders do within our communities. We interpret mysteries. We plumb the depths of the human experience. We hold space for tension and unanswered questions.

When we're at our best in youth ministry, we guide and accompany young people toward making meaning of their lives. When we're not, we shortcut to glib, settled answers, stale narratives, or clever equations for right living—all of which fall short of the kind of faith we hope our students will develop.

Making Meaning Is Like Theological Gardening

Key to making meaning is theological reflection—helping young people explore how God interacts with their story and how they interpret God's action, inaction, and character in light of what happened.

Our Fuller Seminary colleague Scott Cormode has argued that one of the key roles of any type of pastor is to cultivate meaning with people. A pastoral leader must function not only as a decision-making builder or a people-empowering shepherd but also as a meaning-making gardener. Cormode writes,

> The Gardener acknowledges that he can only evoke growth, he can never produce it. The vocabulary that a minister plants in the congregation, the stories that she sows, and the theological categories that she cultivates, bear fruit when the people use those categories to make sense of the world around them.[2]

This approach echoes the apostle Paul: "I planted the seed, Apollos watered it, but God has been making it grow" (1 Cor. 3:6). Like Paul, we cannot know for sure how our theological gardening will turn out, but we can trust the Holy Spirit is at work in our work.

Making Meaning Can Empower Marginalized Teenagers

The action-reflection cycle (introduced in chapter 7) can be subversive.[3] Teenagers form faith and character as they try, reflect, and then try again—going back into everyday life with new tools from learned experience.

Perhaps surprisingly, this cycle has been a critical tool for historically marginalized communities who have oppressively been told how to be, how to live, and what is "normal" and acceptable based on a single perspective—namely, White normativity. Instead, since all discipleship is contextual, diverse communities and young people can be empowered to adapt character development and discipleship through the meaning-making of action and reflection.

Making meaning with young people is best done not through conferring our meaning on them but by asking questions (as Jen emphasized in chapter 6), centering their experiences, and staying curious about our own reflexive responses so we're not defaulting to bias. Giving an experience a name and a meaning is an act of power. Young people are doing this on their own, with or without us. Why *wouldn't* we want to join them? If it's valuable to them, it needs to be valuable to us.

When we give space for young people to exercise this interpretive power—especially those who typically don't experience such power—it can be transformative.

For example, students in one group interview in an urban multiethnic church shared a number of ways their leaders create opportunities for meaning-making experiences. A student recalled a particularly powerful moment when this came together for them: "There was one time we went to a youth retreat and we talked about how we are so different at church than when we're with our friends. At the beginning of the service, they asked us, 'How are you different around others than you are at church?' They gave us paper masks and asked us to write down our answers on the masks. We had worship and a sermon, and I was sobbing at the end of the sermon. We went outside and ripped up our masks and threw them in the fire. Most kids were sobbing, and so were the adult volunteers. It was one of the best moments I've ever had because we were so vulnerable with each other."

As often as possible, meaning-making shouldn't solely come "down" from leaders to students but should be a mutual journey in which students are just as likely to experience the "aha" without leaders needing to make interpretations for them.

Shared Meaning-Making Fosters Identity, Belonging, and Purpose

Political parties, gangs, denominations—these are all meaning-making constructs, telling stories about the way life is, the way life should be, and how we can make it happen. In-groups tell believers what to believe. At times, they demand loyalty not just to the group but to the *narrative*. Making meaning together fosters belonging, sometimes so deep that members give their lives for the shared story.

Psychological research links abstract meaning-making in social environments like faith-based youth groups with a sense of identity, belonging, and overall flourishing. One meta-analysis observes,

> Because thriving involves attitudes and actions that benefit others, the moral beliefs and caring relationships that are usually characteristic of religion and spirituality offer opportunities for constructing meaning that can inform youths' values-aligned goals that motivate prosocial behaviors.[4]

Caring relationships provide critical scaffolding for this internal formation.

In youth ministry, we're pretty good at creating meaning-rich environments. When we gather, our spaces, rituals, songs, words, and ways of being together repeat patterns that reinforce identity and belonging. In our team's research for *3 Big Questions That Change Every Teenager*, we heard young people say they feel like they belong when they share experiences with others.[5] The collective meaning that comes from being on the church softball team, joining the youth choir, or going on a fall retreat can help a student cross the bridge from outsider to insider. And serving together—whether at church, locally, or on mission and service trips—can catalyze purpose.

Three Barriers to Making Meaning

Despite the importance of processing experiences and cultivating meaning with students, youth ministry leaders often skip over this point on the Faith Beyond Youth Group Compass. We do so to our—and teenagers'—detriment. At least three barriers keep us from consistently making meaning.

1. We Lack Time and Practice

If we're honest, most of us feel busy and tired most of the time. It's easy to get overwhelmed by the pace and demands of ministry, which, as we saw in chapter 1, can result in exhaustion and burnout. When we're caught up in the details, we can miss the significant moments with potential to impact a teenager's trajectory.

We can also miss our own meaning-rich moments when we're busy, stressed, and distracted. Similar to modeling growth, reflective practice is essential to being a meaning-making leader. But we have less to offer students if we skip our own growth. When it comes to depth, we can't lead others where we haven't gone ourselves.

2. We Lack Clarity on Issues That Matter to Students

"I'm just seeing a lot of students suffering with anxiety about the future—worried about high school, worried about college," one youth pastor told us. "Their prayers have been different. They pray, 'I hope I get home okay, hope my school won't get shot up, hope I won't get sick.' There's so much racial pain, and they wish it would get better, but I hear hopelessness about that. How do you add hope in the face of all of that from students?"

Like this youth pastor, we may wonder, *How do we add hope?* We believe hope starts when we listen for the real questions and concerns young people care about. Much like Jen's students in chapter 6 who wished she'd teach on subjects that mattered to them, teenagers want and need us to be present with them when they're processing these questions beyond our teaching.

But being present and listening are only the groundwork for making meaning. Young people want help planting, watering, and cultivating seedlings of character that reflect their faith. The problem is, we often lack clarity about some of the topics they really want to talk about.

For example, in my (Brad's) youth ministry, students voiced that while it was clear where our church stood on racial justice and welcoming immigrants, they were frustrated with our church's lack of clear language when it came to sexual and gender identity. "We don't know what adults think about this, and we don't know if some of us or our friends will be accepted here because it's not clear," they said.

They were right. They didn't hear clear messaging because our church didn't have any. We hadn't agreed on language for how we understood these complex issues and how we would respond pastorally to non-heteronormative or non-binary persons.

That lack of clarity makes meaning-making a challenge for volunteers working with students who wonder about current issues and are looking to the church for support—not necessarily to give them settled answers but to listen, open the Bible with them, and help them faithfully wrestle with the complexity.

3. Teenagers Aren't There Yet—or They're Distracted

Raise your hand if you've ever struggled to get a group of sophomore boys to take *any* conversation seriously.

Sometimes I (Brad) plan out an evening of youth group as if the room will be populated by relatively serious, thoughtfully focused *adults*. I craft deep questions and interactive response opportunities (often involving candles, journaling, or some kind of altar—or all three), anticipating profound connection and encounters with God.

Then our *actual* students show up. Some are tired, others distracted—by life or by their phones[6]—and still others came only because their parents wanted them there. The students who are excited to attend might mostly want to talk to an old friend, flirt with a new friend, let off steam, or just get out of the house. Some really want to be seen or to have a chance to talk about their week with someone who will genuinely listen. What's more, their brains are still forming the capacity to make meaning from abstract ideas.[7]

Sure, a few of our students might be eager to connect with God, hear a life-altering message, or be mind-blown by Bible study. But these are secondary motivations (at best) for most. Who can blame them for being, well, teenagers?

On all kinds of levels, I end up missing students by expecting more than they're willing—or perhaps able—to give to youth group on any given night.

How Jesus Made Meaning

As with all the previous points on the Faith Beyond Youth Group Compass, Jesus has walked this landscape before us, and its topography reveals a God-with-us who made meaning in subversive, surprising moves.

Jesus Was Known for Flipping Scripts

One of the ways Jesus made meaning with people was by changing the narrative. Jesus knew that people tend to hold relatively fixed views of the world and interpretations of Scripture. His teachings and actions consistently challenged common understanding and seemed to suggest that our concept of God may be too small.

This is especially true for those he encountered personally. Think about the way he flipped the script for the woman being publicly shamed for adultery—and for her accusers (John 8:1–11). Everyone likely expected Jesus to condemn her for her character failure or, if not, to fight with the religious leaders. Instead, he does something no one anticipated: he is silent. Then he mic-drops, "Let any one of you who is without sin be the first to throw a stone at her" (v. 7). The accusers walk away until only Jesus and the woman remain. Finally,

> Jesus [straightens] up and asked her, "Woman, where are they? Has no one condemned you?"
>
> "No one, sir," she [says].
>
> "Then neither do I condemn you," Jesus [declares]. "Go now and leave your life of sin." (vv. 10–11)

Jesus was gentle with this woman's story, firm with demons when he commanded them to return people to themselves, and dramatic in his encounter with Saul on the road to Damascus. But every time, Jesus freed people from false stories and helped them make better meaning—truer meaning—of their lives.

Jesus Reoriented His Followers to See Common Things in Uncommon Ways

Those of us who love words tend to think meaning is about a new vocabulary. That's not how Jesus made meaning most of the time. He built on words and domains his listeners knew well, in stories mostly about food, families, and farming. Then he brought new meaning to these common words and images. He said, "The kingdom of God is like . . ."

a farmer who scatters seed
a woman who finds a lost coin
a father who finds a lost son

And, "I am . . ."

the light of the world
the bread of life
the vine
the good shepherd

Part of the *goodness* of the Good News is that the kingdom of God is accessible—though hidden, it's also obvious. It's at hand. Among us now.

Jesus Used Symbols and Actions to Make Meaning

Not only did Jesus make meaning through his stories and teaching but he also used symbols and actions. He invited fishermen to throw their nets on the other side of the boat, to cast out into deep waters, and even to leave their nets and boats behind because he would teach them how to fish in a whole new way.

Jesus broke bread, poured wine, and shared with his disciples. This ritual meal has endured as one of the most meaning-packed practices of the church across time.

And, of course, Jesus allowed his own body to be beaten, humiliated, nailed to wood, and lifted up in shameful political and religious execution, all for the love of humanity. The way Jesus died was so significant that the image of the Roman cross is one of the most universally recognized religious symbols in the world.

Jesus Made Meaning Out of Tragic Loss

"Faith is not knowing, or even committing to, information or religious participation but is rather experiencing the very narrative shape of your life through the experience of cross and resurrection. To pass on faith . . . is inviting the young and old to interpret the story of their lives through the cross and resurrection of the person of Jesus." —Andrew Root[8]

Prior to his own death, Jesus met others in suffering, grief, and loss. He compassionately raised a daughter to life at the request of a desperate father, and he interrupted a funeral procession to bring a son to life for a grieving mother.

Jesus met his close friends Martha and Mary in their devastation at the loss of their brother, Lazarus. Jesus was so moved by their grief that he wept—even though he knew their dead brother would be restored in just a few moments. While Jesus was fully capable of escaping all physical and emotional pain, he chose not to. He grieved, he experienced betrayal from a close friend, and he walked through death—the ultimate human loss—as one who relentlessly chose to identify with our sufferings. For Jesus, as for us, the suffering and the meaning are intermingled.

Jesus not only performed miraculous healings but also filled these experiences with spiritual meaning for those who witnessed them. In the case of Lazarus' siblings, Jesus reveals to Martha, "I am the resurrection and the life. The one who believes in me will live, even though they die; and whoever lives by believing in me will never die" (John 11:25–26). He does not deny death but offers a way to reach for hope beyond it.

Following Jesus' own traumatic death, his friends grapple with hard questions—including what to make of Jesus' claims, like the one he'd made to Martha. While two of them walk together away from Jerusalem toward Emmaus (Luke 24:13–35), the resurrected Jesus appears, disguised, alongside them. In the midst of their disorientation, he helps them process what happened and make meaning from it. Jesus ultimately reveals himself while at the table, again blessing, breaking, and giving them bread.

Navigational Tools for Making Meaning

> "We're very intentional with language—we say this kind of stuff over and over again. When we release seniors to college, we talk about: this is home, this is always your place. You can always come back home, and you will always have a place in this family no matter what happens. You belong here."

Intentional is music to our ears (it's one of Kara's favorite words!). If making meaning is about anything, it's about being intentional. We aren't doing the work of ministry flippantly. We aren't just "hanging out" with teenagers or "supervising" or—worse—"chaperoning" them (even if your actual title is "youth chaperone"). Your time with young people is so valuable; being intentional with that time can make it transformational.

Based on our research and ideas from youth ministries like yours, here are navigational tools you can use to orient your Faith Beyond Youth Group Compass toward making meaning.

Give Everything a "Why"

Recently, we were launching into our middle school ministry team meeting to plan for fall Sunday night youth group, and I (Brad) had a long list we needed to work through. But one leader jumped in and asked, "Can someone remind us why we do Sunday night youth group? What's the purpose?"

For a second, I was annoyed. (My list! My list!)

But then I was glad he asked. Though it was only a short diversion from our meeting agenda, the question gave our seasoned leaders a chance to share what they thought was most important about this ministry gathering and gave our new volunteers the opportunity to catch the vision more clearly.

That's because starting with "why" is critical to meaning.[9]

One antidote to churning out "good kids" with inconsequential faith lies in giving them a "why" for all you do in youth ministry. As I was reminded in that meeting, this starts with first making sure you and your team know the purpose behind your ministry's work.

Better yet, we can ask students what *they think* the purpose of a given activity, program, structure, or trip might be. Their answers could surprise us and open up great conversations!

A meaning mismatch could mean you need a realignment about purpose. It could also mean it's time to retire a program, change up an activity, or rethink a trip you've repeated for ages.

Identify Values

Harvard psychologist Susan David writes, "When you connect to your real self and what you believe to be important, the gulf between how you feel and how you behave closes up."[10] This finding from David's work on "emotional agility" might be key to helping some teenagers bridge the character gap through identifying their values. Through a faith beyond youth group lens, we might think about this as discovering and choosing Christ-oriented values to live by, and then acting based on those values.

Research shows that this kind of chosen value-based behavior isn't just behavior modification—or worse, behavior-based faith—but is actually the kind of change rooted in meaning.

Deeply held values are freely chosen, are ongoing, guide choices, and foster self-acceptance.[11] To explore values with students, consider having them ask themselves some of the following questions as journaling and discussion prompts in small groups, a retreat setting, or one-on-one mentoring.[12]

Deep down, what matters to me?

What relationships do I want to build? Who are the people who matter most in my life?

What do I want my life to be about?

How do I feel most of the time? What kinds of situations make me feel most alive?

If a miracle wiped out all the anxiety and stress in my life, what would my life look like? What new things would I want to pursue?

Based on these answers, what are some of my personal values? How do I hope they guide my life now and in the future?

Use Meaning-Making Conversation Tools

"So often the experiences that define us are the ones we didn't pick."
—Kate Bowler[13]

Tragedy disorients. For those of us who have ministered through crises such as natural disasters, racialized violence, a school shooting, or the death of a student in our ministry, it can be paralyzing to decide what to do next.

What should youth group look like tomorrow night after the suicide of a local student this week? What do students need to hear, pray, and do in the face of great pain? Practically, meaning-making in ministry can look like taking opportunities to process with students:

1. *What happened?* Listen to students' accounts of their experiences. Stay curious and ask follow-up questions rather than assuming you understand. Suspend judgment. Ask them to identify how they're feeling.

2. *What does it mean?* Help them get curious as they interpret personal, local, or global events. Wonder with them about what their experiences mean through the lens of their faith.

3. *What now?* Encourage them to identify simple next steps to help them move forward with new meaning and a new connection to God and to God's people. *What might God be inviting you into?*

Many teenagers are looking for help to tie their faith to purpose through activism and justice-seeking. They hope we'll show up with them to march and demonstrate, and when we do, we can model "praying with our feet" to connect the dots between faith and action.

Others are struggling with very personal conflict, confusion, loss, addiction, or abuse. With these young people, we need to be mindful about when to refer to a professional (in general, when the situation feels beyond our training and competence to help, when the young person is in danger, or when they could be dangerous to themselves or others).

We also must be mindful not to jump to a "God answer" for every situation. Teenagers who are wading through waters of pain and loss might not yet be ready to hear how God might be with them, or "what Scripture says," or anything that may sound trite or dismissive of their actual experience. Our well-intended but poorly timed meaning-making can end up feeling like we're shoving their heads under the water rather than coming alongside to buoy them up.

Instead, these moments call for the ministry of presence and accompaniment—just being with a young person in their hurt. Sometimes the deepest meaning can emerge from saying nothing at all.

Getting Your Students the Help They Need

Teenagers who are struggling with anxiety, depression, self-harm, or suicidal ideation may need connections with professional counselors and therapists for additional support. If you're worried about the safety of a teenager you know, contact the National Suicide Prevention Lifeline right away: call or text 988 or 1-800-273-TALK, or visit 988LifeLine.org.

In addition, the Steve Fund Crisis Text Line is dedicated to the mental health and emotional well-being of students of color and can be reached by texting STEVE to 741-741 or by visiting SteveFund.org/CrisisTextLine.

If you need help finding local mental health professionals for young people, try asking pastors or nearby schools for their recommendations. Because we know cost can be a barrier to accessing mental healthcare, consider how your church can financially support families. Many of the churches we know offer scholarships to help families access therapy and other mental health support they need. Others work with providers who offer their services on a sliding scale.

Reflect and Debrief Both during and after Service and Mission Work

Over a dozen years ago, our FYI team partnered with researchers, cultural intelligence experts, and short-term missions agency leaders from around the country to develop a new model for making meaning with students through service and mission work.[14] In an ideal meaning-making service experience, support and feedback surround students during action and reflection. *Support* provides safety for students to keep trying even when they flounder, and *feedback* offers new insights to their experiences along the way.

Here's how it works: As young people are being purposefully stretched by their encounters, they are constantly assigning internal meaning to those experiences. These inner conversations rarely stop, as their brains work overtime to process the often-disjointed perspectives they tumble through each day. The goals of reflecting and debriefing are to help decipher these messages and give them lasting meaning, while support and feedback provide the backdrop for this drama. As it unfolds, trusted adults are somewhat like stage managers, giving cues and offering encouragement.

As stage managers, we can structure our service and mission work for meaning-making in a few practical ways:

- *Maximize support channels*, increasing the number of adults scaffolding students before, during, and after their experiences.
- *Create opportunities for risk*, including the chance to stretch and even fail as part of the learning process.
- *Reflect back what you see*, being specific about what character traits you notice underneath students' behaviors and what you appreciate about who they are (not just what they do).
- *Level the playing field*, equalizing power between leaders and students as much as possible, bringing teenagers into decision-making, and ensuring leaders and students alike share in the same kinds of basic labor.
- *Hold back on bailing students out*, resisting the temptation to save them from hitting a challenging moment, a cultural wall, or the consequences of a poor decision.
- *Plan time for personal and group reflection and debriefing*, both during the experience and when it's over. This helps young people make long-term meaning from their in-the-moment responses and interpretations.

Help Students Learn to Tell a Better Story

John Dewey famously quipped, "We do not learn from experience. We learn from reflecting on experience."[15] In other words, experiences don't teach us or shape us on their own— they shape us by the stories we tell afterward. We need to employ storytelling not only to teach but also to help our students learn to tell better stories about their lives and about our shared life as people who follow Jesus.

There are a lot of bad stories out there.

In our research for *3 Big Questions That Shape Every Teenager*, we found that young people often tell incomplete, unhelpful, or downright toxic stories about their identity, belonging, and purpose. Our hope is that the Faith Beyond Youth Group Compass can be a way you lead them toward better stories—Christ-centered stories—about their lives.

As we noted in chapter 2, young people are forming faith in an age of (often well-earned) critical press and low public opinion about churches and faith leaders. In the midst of this environment, we can help them tell a better story about the church—but only if they've experienced it.

Good storytelling helps young people integrate and interpret their stories in light of the Jesus story and the stories of God's people. We reflect together so teenagers can go back into the world with a fresh cut of their better story.

Consider these navigational tools for meaning-making through storytelling:

- *Notice what gets repeated.* What are the Scripture verses, sayings, and adages that shape you, your students, your church, or your tradition? Where did they originate? What worldview are they championing? Are there any you want to stop repeating, or others you want to repeat more often?

- *Tell local stories and cultural stories.* Yale religious scholar Almeda Wright emphasizes the importance in African American churches and communities of retelling historical stories to boost the resilience of young people as they face challenges today. Young people need to be reminded about "the legacy of faith, resistance, survival, and liberation that permeates their communities of origin . . . such that they not only learn or know the history but that they begin to see the narrative as *their own*."[16]

- *Share testimonies.* In addition to being a powerful teaching tool, testimony narrates faith journeys, growth, and how people in your church make meaning of their lives in light of God's presence and activity.

- *Stop telling cynical stories about the church.* Be mindful about your own frustrations with the church—your specific congregation, the church in the US, or the church across time or continents. As youth leaders, we often find ourselves in periods of struggle and deconstruction of what we thought we knew, believed, or trusted. In the midst of this, we need to find our own safe places to process without passing along our church baggage to our students. We can be honest about the past, lament the failures of God's people across time, and stare collective sin in the face without giving up on the church as God's idea.

Use Objects as Symbols to Make Meaning with Students

Just as Jesus used everyday objects and familiar patterns to make meaning, we can do the same with students. Create ways for teenagers to use their bodies to move, create, build, consider, and pray using objects that become symbolic with spiritual meaning.

- *Oil and sand.* In Scripture, we read about oil as a sign of blessing and sand most often associated with the desert, a place of struggle. Veteran youth worker Michael Mata shared this idea with me (Brad) years ago, and it became a staple in our youth ministry. Near the start of each gathering, we pass around two bottles: one filled with olive oil, the other with sand. Whoever is holding the bottles gets to share one "oil," a blessing or a good thing from the week, and one "sand," a gritty frustration or discouragement from the week.

- *Rocks.* The Old Testament is full of stories of people who set up rocks as altars to designate significant moments and places. Most often, they were altars of remembrance to mark God's faithfulness. Sometimes they were altars of sacrifice, places to make offerings or commitments to God. In the New Testament, we read about Peter being called "rock"; Jesus being named the "stone the builders rejected" which has become the "cornerstone"; and the stone being rolled away from Jesus' tomb. Pick one of these meanings and invite students to utilize rocks to physically build an altar, place a stone of remembrance of God's faithfulness, or remember Jesus' sacrifice.

- *Candles.* Lighting a candle as a symbol of prayer has remained a significant practice across many church traditions over the centuries. Invite students to light candles as they offer prayers (silently or out loud), light candles that can safely be carried while walking during prayer vigils, or light three candles at the start of each gathering to remember the presence of the Trinity in your midst.

- *Water.* Wherever there's water, there is potential for spiritual meaning. In Scripture, water represents chaos, power, death, cleansing, healing, and, of course, baptism—the symbolic death and resurrection ritual that marks Christian identity. Not to mention wells, streams of living water, and the experience of thirst. Tap into any of these meanings through using water interactively with students.

- *Crosses.* At the risk of sounding cliché, making crosses is still a meaningful practice! Engage students in creating or painting a cross in your youth ministry space or sanctuary, give them tiny crosses to carry in their pockets during Lent, or invite them to bring flowers to cover a wooden cross with beautiful colors on Easter.

We Need Young Adult Ministry—Now

Making meaning certainly doesn't stop when high school ends; in fact, it ramps up! Unfortunately, too many of us usher young people out the door of our youth rooms with little direction for what to do next.

They need adults to walk with them into young adulthood, where their meaning questions become deeper, heavier, and more urgent.

Walking with them may mean you or some in your church keep up with them by checking in after they graduate from high school and work at a job, start college, join the military, or take a gap year.

FYI has developed a series of resources to help you support young adults, including an ebook by Steve Argue titled *Young Adult Ministry Now.* Find out more at FullerYouthInstitute.org.

Refined by Fire

The first church I (Brad) formally served was the Methodist church I grew up attending off and on. It wasn't until I was back serving as a youth director (leading students barely younger than me) that I learned more of the church's history. Some of the more seasoned members would mention "the fire" from time to time, and eventually, I learned the story.

A couple of decades beforehand, the church building had been a target of arson around 3 a.m. Elders could still talk about the night they stood across the street and watched as the flames leaped into the early morning winter sky, nearly burning the building to the ground.

The fire happened in the late '70s, and the trend at the time was for downtown churches to move out to the suburbs to build new, expansive campuses with "family activity centers" and large worship spaces to welcome "seekers"—code for young families with kids. Despite this allure, the church's leadership felt a differ-ent kind of resolve. In the wake of the fire, they quickly decided to remain downtown. They sensed God leading them to be a church located in the heart of the community, not the suburbs.

So they raised money and rebuilt from the ashes. They reori-ented the sanctuary and added a balcony to accommodate more worshipers. They preserved a front yard and much of the brick infrastructure, and they even kept the majority of the stained glass window panels depicting Jesus "knocking at the door," despite the brown flame marks that commemorated the trial they had survived.

While I was serving as youth director two decades later, the church went through a process of clarifying its purpose and reimagining its mission for the future. Young people within our youth ministry were part of this process, as were older generations—including those present for the fire and rebuilding.

One of the beautiful elements of that process was story-telling about the past. Over and over, tales of the fire relayed the sense of togetherness that accompanied the rebuilding phase. As we worked to craft a new mission statement, the phrase "refined by fire" bubbled to the surface.

Yes, the story was decades in the past. But it was also part of the present. Being refined by fire meant we could let go of trappings that might keep us stuck in old ways in order to open ourselves to the newness of the future. Weaving "refined by fire" into our mission also ensured that the story would be told across generations, which both encouraged the older members who had invested so much in rebuilding and inspired the younger members who hadn't been born until after that labor of love had long been completed.

The students in our church knew that their congregation drew significant meaning and a sense of purpose from being reborn from the ashes of devastation. This inspired them to find their own part in the story of what God is doing from generation to generation. In fact, the story loaned young people some resilience of their own to carry their faith beyond youth group.

For three of our students in that season (from three different families), being refined by fire meant losing a parent. For a couple of others, it meant walking through recovery for eating disorders. For one high schooler, it meant having a baby her senior year. For another, it meant watching her dad go to jail her senior year. And for me as their youth leader, it meant navigating my dad's paralysis after a severe spinal cord injury.

We all struggled to find meaning through those hard patches. What we shared in common was a faith community in which to walk together toward hope. As you help students uncover meaning from their past and present trials, you will see God nurture character and faith that reach long beyond high school.

REFLECTION QUESTIONS

1. What's compelling to you about the meaning-making aspect of youth ministry?

2. Who are the meaning-makers you gravitate toward or find most helpful to make sense of life and/or faith?

3. Which of the barriers to making meaning—lack of time and practice, lack of clarity on issues young people care about, or lack of student engagement—do you struggle with most?

4. Which of Jesus' meaning-making strategies are most natural to you, and which might be a stretch?

5. What conversation tools could help adults in your ministry better connect with students when they are trying to make meaning of significant events in their lives?

6. In what ways could you strengthen the meaning-making elements of your service and mission work?

YOUR OWN MAP

Charting Faith Beyond YOUR Youth Group

Character is shaped on multiple levels, but the person of character has integrated those levels into a whole personality. The person of character can be counted upon to be reliable and predictable over time. He or she is stable in the face of moral temptation, and chooses right even when it is painful. A person of character responds authentically to value; her loves are ordered. To have character is to refuse anything that satisfies one's lower loves. It is to put aside our natural tendency toward pride and selfishness, and to seek instead the good of others, of a community, of country.

Anne Snyder[1]

One of my (Kara's) most vivid recent encounters with young people was on a snowy day in Colorado. As a Southern Californian, I see snow only a handful of times per year—and usually that snow is already on the ground. When the cold white stuff is actually *descending from the sky*, that's extra special.

I love seeing snow fall—from the comfort of the great (warm) indoors. When it started snowing during a recent two-day trip to Colorado Springs a few months ago, I looked for every way possible to stay inside.

To my delight, as I drove around the corner to a nearby coffee shop, it had a drive-thru option. When I pulled up to the window to grab my chai tea latte, the young barista who leaned out the window to greet me was smiling. More like beaming. Chuckling, she enthusiastically welcomed me, "Thanks for coming to our coffee shop. We'll have your drink ready in a minute."

I've been to more than my fair share of coffee shops. This employee was in the upper 10 percent of friendliness and hospitality—all while snow fell all around her. And on her.

Intrigued by her cheeriness, I looked past her to the interior of the store. Like the drive-thru greeter, the other baristas were joyful. One was handing a drink to another, and a third was animated as she shared a story while blending a drink.

In the ninety seconds I waited at the window, I observed some magical teamwork. The four young team members were helping each other. Talking. Laughing. Cooperating. Enjoying their work. Giving each other high fives.

These coworkers were linked by a sense of mutual belonging. That camaraderie, as well as their shared mission to serve customers, seemed to instill a clear and passionate purpose. The part they were playing in turning that mission into reality appeared to give them pride and a sense of identity.

As I rolled out of the parking lot with my latte, I thought, *What a great coffee shop. What teenager wouldn't want to work there?*

I had driven only about a half a block when I then thought to myself, *Wait. Why can't* the church *be like that for young people?*

If a meager faith is what we're giving young people, no wonder they're leaving the church. As wise friend, adviser, and youth ministry scholar Montague Williams has said in various settings, "Young people are leaving church to *find church*."

Plotting Where to Go from Here

We want churches in your community to be the most life-giving hubs for young people—far more generative than even the liveliest coffee shop. We believe your church can cultivate character and give students a Jesus-centered identity, belonging, and purpose that change how they view themselves and our world. We think that can be true not just during your weekend worship services or youth group meetings but all week long.

But the energy I saw in that coffee shop doesn't happen by accident. There was certainly a store manager who cast a vision for the type of service the staff could provide, supplied training in how to work together as a high-functioning team, and likely promoted honest discussions that created a sense of community.

Similarly, helping your students develop character and faith beyond youth group takes leadership. It also involves God's blessing, training, time, energy, resources, and hard work.

As well as a map.

We don't feel right equipping you with the five points of the Faith Beyond Youth Group Compass without also equipping you with a map.

We know young people, but *you know your young people*. All ministry happens in a context, and you know your context best. We are committed to helping you develop a plan that works for your setting and your students.

As motivated as you are to lead your ministry forward, we want to help you plot a map that pinpoints the strategic areas that provide the most discipleship leverage. Additionally, we want your plan to identify doable next steps and help you identify teenagers and other adults who can walk with you on your ministry's character-building journey.

Finally, we believe that all of life and leadership is God's curriculum to keep teaching and transforming us. We want your map to reflect the ministry reality that God wants to work not only through you but also in you.

Measuring Your Progress Using the Faith Beyond Youth Group Compass

A good plan starts with knowing where you are—or with what beloved former Fuller Seminary trustee Max De Pree labeled as the first job of leaders, which is to "define reality."[2]

As researchers and leaders, we've noticed that what matters most in assessing youth ministry reality isn't what we as adults think but what teenagers think. So before creating your map, answer the thirty questions below through the lens of your students to measure your ministry's progress on each of the five points of the Faith Beyond Youth Group Compass.

You can score your ministry by yourself. But it is probably much better if you ask a few teenagers, youth group graduates, parents, and/or youth ministry volunteers for their input. In fact, ideally you would ask a diverse cross section of your students to answer these questions to unearth any gaps between your perceptions and their actual experiences. As we've noted throughout the book, listening is important—this approach could provide you another forum to listen well.

Cultivate Trust

On a scale of 1–5, with 5 being "very strongly," how strongly would the teenagers in your ministry agree with the following statements related to *cultivating trust*:

1. We can share our significant feelings and experiences in youth group.

    1················2················3················4················5

2. When we share significant feelings and experiences in youth group, we can trust the adults to act in our best interest.

    1················2················3················4················5

3. We feel relationally close to others in our youth ministry.

    1················2················3················4················5

4. Our relationships in our youth ministry have been consistent over time.

    1················2················3················4················5

5. Adults in our youth ministry empathize with what we're experiencing, meaning they notice and care.

    1················2················3················4················5

6. Adults in our youth ministry show us who they authentically are—instead of trying to be somebody they aren't.

    1················2················3················4················5

Total score for this point of the Faith Beyond Youth Group Compass: _____

Model Growth

On a scale of 1–5, with 5 being "very strongly," how strongly would the teenagers in your ministry agree with the following statements related to *modeling growth*:

1. We are around adults whose character inspires us to imitate them.

   1················2················3················4················5

2. Adults in our youth ministry model personal growth.

   1················2················3················4················5

3. Adults in our youth ministry model spiritual growth.

   1················2················3················4················5

4. Introverts feel seen and valued in our youth ministry as much as extroverts.

   1················2················3················4················5

5. We're regularly encouraged to model our lives after Jesus' example.

   1················2················3················4················5

6. It's natural in our youth ministry to talk about changing and growing over time.

   1················2················3················4················5

Total score for this point of the Faith Beyond Youth Group Compass: _____

Teach for Transformation

On a scale of 1–5, with 5 being "very strongly," how strongly would the teenagers in your ministry agree with the following statements related to *teaching for transformation*:

1. We can identify rituals and practices that are used in both our youth ministry and our larger faith community.

   1················2················3················4················5

2. Adults and teens regularly share stories with each other in our youth ministry.

   1················2················3················4················5

3. Adults in our youth ministry know what topics and issues we care about most.

   1················2················3················4················5

4. Our leaders regularly use questions to teach.

   1················2················3················4················5

5. My peers and I regularly teach in our youth ministry.

   1················2················3················4················5

6. Adult leaders in our youth ministry willingly share their authority with us.

   1················2················3················4················5

Total score for this point of the Faith Beyond Youth Group Compass: _____

Practice Together

On a scale of 1–5, with 5 being "very strongly," how strongly would the teenagers in your ministry agree with the following statements related to *practicing together*:

1. Our youth ministry gives us regular opportunities to practice loving each other and our world.

   1............2............3............4............5

2. When we practice loving others, we do so in community —with others.

   1............2............3............4............5

3. Our youth ministry not just helps us think about character with our minds but actually gives us opportunities to feel and act lovingly.

   1............2............3............4............5

4. We use current events as springboards to cultivate character.

   1............2............3............4............5

5. We have opportunities to lead and use our gifts to cultivate character in ourselves and others.

   1............2............3............4............5

6. The adults who serve in our youth ministry practice loving others even when they are not with us.

   1............2............3............4............5

Total score for this point of the Faith Beyond Youth Group Compass: _____

Make Meaning

On a scale of 1–5, with 5 being "very strongly," how strongly would the teenagers in your ministry agree with the following statements related to *making meaning*:

1. Our youth ministry intentionally gives time and space to process and make meaning from experiences.

    1················2················3················4················5

2. Adults in our youth ministry ask good questions to help us find meaning from significant events in our lives.

    1················2················3················4················5

3. We use symbols, stories, and everyday objects to make spiritual meaning and explore faith in our youth ministry.

    1················2················3················4················5

4. We have clarity on what our church believes about current issues that matter to us.

    1················2················3················4················5

5. Our youth ministry makes spiritual meaning in the midst of tragedy and loss.

    1················2················3················4················5

6. We regularly process how we are learning and growing from our service and mission experiences.

    1················2················3················4················5

Total score for this point of the Faith Beyond Youth Group Compass: _____

Choose 1–2 Points on the Faith Beyond Youth Group Compass

Now compare your scores on all five points of the Faith Beyond Youth Group Compass. Given your scores, which one or two points do you want to focus on first? You may want to select the areas where your scores—or those of your students—are lowest. Or you may want to choose the one or two points that most resonated with you throughout this book.

Charting Your Map Forward

Congratulations! You have now identified your focus on the Faith Beyond Youth Group Compass. Now it's time to prayerfully identify other key details to chart your map forward.

Who Can Accompany You on Your Journey?

1. Which other adults serving in your youth ministry would want to help build faith beyond youth group?

2. Which parents could help support your new commitment to building character?

3. Which students would be interested in being part of these adventures?

4. Who among senior leadership in your church (such as pastors, church board members, or other key congregational leaders) would it be helpful to involve?

5. When could you bring these folks together to share this vision, discuss the results from the survey above, and brainstorm some next steps?

What Are Some Possible Next Steps?

In our FYI training cohorts, we accompany leaders like you through an extensive change process that offers even more support and tangible action steps forward. To find out more about how your church can benefit from additional training, visit FaithBeyondYouthGroup.org.

While the best maps are usually developed with the input of others, it's not too early to start identifying your best next steps. Feel free to review relevant previous chapters for ideas as you jot down answers to the following questions.

In this exercise, keep in mind what you learned about your ministry's alignment with the Faith Beyond Youth Group Compass and try to be as specific as you can in your answers. If possible, write down who will be responsible for each action step.

1. What can your ministry do in the *next three days* to make progress in this area of faith beyond youth group?

2. How about the *next three weeks*?

3. What about the *next three months*?

4. What resistance might you meet as you try to take these steps?

5. How can you lovingly and effectively respond to that resistance?

How Can This Journey Change You?

1. How might God be inviting you to grow as a leader as you focus on building character and faith beyond youth group?

2. What might God want to show you about your own faith or relationship with God during this next season?

3. What spiritual practices or personal habits can help you stay open to hearing from God and learning the lessons God has for you?

Empowering Young People to Guide Us Forward

As I (Kara) was running errands one weekend afternoon with my daughter, Krista, she shared the type of church she wanted to be part of after college. At age twenty, she's been working on what faith beyond youth group looks like for her. "I want to be part of a church that's more welcoming and inclusive than most churches are today," she said.

I affirmed this hunger for a loving community, which prompted Krista to muse, "I guess I'll just have to wait for all the old people to die off for our church to be like that."

It's a good thing we were already stopped at a red light because I think I would have automatically slammed on the brakes. "No, no, no," I begged Krista. "Please don't say that. The church needs young people like you to lead us forward in new ways of loving Jesus and loving others. It's young people like you who can lead us in a love and justice revolution."

Admittedly, it's not enough for us as adults to *say* we want teenagers to lead us in changing the church for the better. We have to invite and give young people the space to actually do so. We have to grant them the freedom they need to pursue character and cultivate faith.

That's what Jesus did.

That's what we've seen leaders across the country do.

That's what we know you can do.

That's a faith beyond youth group—faith that lasts for a teenager's entire week and their entire life.

Acknowledgments

This book represents the fruit of four years of intensive research, informed by a treasure trove of insights amassed over nearly twenty years from investigations conducted by the Fuller Youth Institute (FYI) team and numerous partners. It also represents learning from the combined decades of youth ministry the three of us have logged, as well as the many leaders who entrusted their stories to us for the sake of this project and for the love of "youth group" in all its expressions. To that end, we owe immense gratitude to a cloud of witnesses (Heb. 12:1) far too great to name here.

As with every FYI project, this one would have been impossible without the dedication of its core research team. Very special thanks go to Tyler Greenway, FYI's research director during the majority of this project, for his leadership and expertise, as well as Aaron Yenney and Lisa Nopachai, whose seasons at FYI focused on this particular grant but whose influence spread much wider and deeper. Amy Carnall assisted tremendously in the final research steps and in compiling stories for this book and tirelessly hunting down leads, quotes, additional literature reviews, and citations. We simply could not have completed the project without her! Additional key researchers included Miriam Cho (whose untimely death our team is still grieving), Lisa Hanle, Roslyn Hernández, Quanesha Moore, Levi Price, Gabriella Silva, Elizabeth Tamez Méndez (who served multiple roles as adviser, researcher, and contributor to chapter 5), and Yulee Lee (who contributed to early outlines of this book and authored chapter 7).

Further support for the project in its various stages was provided by Daniel Alvarado, Stephen Bay, Taylor Cockrell, Abigayle Craigg, Own Her, Patrick Jacques, Jessica Lopez, Lauren Mulder, Joyce Oh, and Mary Yeboah. We're also incredibly grateful to all those who nominated participants for this research.

A number of folks contributed valuable input along the way, whether through participating in an early research summit, advising, expanding the work through resource subgrants, or pre-reading an early version of the manuscript to provide vital feedback. We would've learned half as much if we hadn't had help from Lauren Amstutz, Steven Argue, Jeffrey Bamaca, Jonathan Banks (who also contributed an interview to chapter 4), Marcos Canales, Michael Paul Cartledge, Kendall Cotton Bronk, Kenda Creasy Dean, Steven Christoforou, Steven Dang, Joyce del Rosario, Rachel Dodd, Lindsay Dorman, Zach Ellis, Sarah Farmer, Lisette Fraser, Tommy Givens, Perry Hawkins, Garrison Hayes, Sarah Henry, Jane Hong-Guzmán de León, InJoon Hur, Kristen Ivy, Alexander James, Reggie Joiner, Andy Jung, Chris Kim, James King, Mike King, Crystal Kirgiss, Deech Kirk, Eileen Kooreman, Phil Lewis, Ahren Martinez, Meredith Miller, Jeremy Morelock, Jake Mulder, Tommy Nixon, John

Park, Justin Pickard, Erin Raffety, Jonathan Reynolds, Gene Roehlkepartain, Andy Root, Abigail Rusert, Sarah Schnitker, Brett Talley, Chelsy Tyler, Virginia Ward, Pete Watts, Montague Williams, Chris Wilterdink, and Almeda Wright.

Special thanks to Macy Phenix Davis for the brilliant cover design and creative direction.

As ever, we are grateful to the FYI and TENx10 team members not already mentioned above who have supported this work in various ways by their faithful service, including Nasim Bowlus, Raymond Chang, Charissa Dornbush, Jennifer Guerra Aldana, Nica Halula, Jennifer Hananouchi, Chuck Hunt, Issac Kim, John Kwok, Will Lewis, Erik Francisco Medina-Nieves, LaTasha Nesbitt, Giovanny Panginda, Caleb Roose, Hannah Struwe, and Vanesa Zuleta Goldberg. We're also grateful for the ways the broader Fuller Seminary community and senior leadership enrich our work and stand behind our mission.

Deep gratitude goes to our editor, Stephanie Duncan Smith, for pushing us toward clarity through the writing process time and again and for being patient with our numerous trials and setbacks until we made it to the finish line together. The publishing team at Baker Books continues to be such a great partner, and we're so grateful to Brianna DeWitt and the marketing and publicity team for again preparing us so well for launch. As always, Greg Johnson at WordServe Literary has been a joy to work with from idea phase to publication.

We are so very thankful for the generous funders who make FYI research and resources possible, and this project could not have happened without the support of the John Templeton Foundation and the enthusiastic encouragement of Richard Bollinger.

Finally, our families keep us going and make it possible for us to do the hard work of bringing a book into the world. None of us could have guessed half of the obstacles that threatened to undo us over the course of writing this one. Our spouses and children provided faithful support through countless untold acts—from tiny to monumental—that made all the difference. We're beyond grateful for Dave, Nathan, Krista, and Jessica Powell; Doug, Hope, and Kendall Bradbury; and Missy, Anna, Kara, and Joel Griffin.

Notes

Chapter 1 Character

1. Ying Chen and Tyler J. VanderWeele, "Associations of Religious Upbringing with Subsequent Health and Well-Being from Adolescence to Young Adulthood: An Outcome-Wide Analysis," *American Journal of Epidemiology* 187, no. 11 (November 2018): 2355–64.

2. Jessica Halliday Hardie, Lisa D. Pearce, and Melissa Lundquist Denton, "The Dynamics and Correlates of Religious Service Attendance in Adolescence," *Youth and Society* 48, no. 2 (March 2016): 151–75, https://www.ncbi.nlm.nih.gov/pmc/articles/PMC4758987/.

3. The Barna Group, "New Research Explores the Long-Term Effect of Spiritual Activity Among Children and Teens," Barna, November 16, 2009, https://www.barna.com/research/new-research-explores-the-long-term-effect-of-spiritual-activity-among-children-and-teens/.

4. Our estimate that 40 to 50 percent of high school graduates will fail to stick with their faith is based on a compilation of data from various studies, dating back to several studies with Millennial young people—most notably detailed in the 2011 book by David Kinnaman and Aly Hawkins, *You Lost Me* (Grand Rapids: Baker Books, 2011), as well as the National Study of Youth and Religion's findings in Christian Smith with Patricia Snell, *Souls in Transition: The Religious and Spiritual Lives of Emerging Adults* (New York: Oxford University Press, 2009), 109–10. In a more recent compilation of research highlighted in "The Great Opportunity Report," 42 million young people are expected to leave the Christian church (across Roman Catholic, mainline, and evangelical traditions) between 2020 and 2050. See Pinetops Foundation, "The Great Opportunity Report," 2018, www.greatopportunity.org.

5. The Barna Group, "Adults Who Attended Church as Children Show Lifelong Effects," Barna, November 5, 2001, https://www.barna.com/research/adults-who-attended-church-as-children-show-lifelong-effects/.

6. Pinetops Foundation, "The Great Opportunity Report."

7. The Barna Group, "Pastors Share Top Reasons They've Considered Quitting Ministry in the Past Year," Barna, April 27, 2022, https://www.barna.com/research/pastors-quitting-ministry/.

8. The Youth Cartel and Jeremiah Project, "2022 Youth Worker Well-Being Report," Youth Cartel, accessed March 20, 2023, 3, https://theyouthcartel.com/blog/2022-youth-worker-well-being-report.

9. Liz Wiseman, "Is Your Burnout from Too Much Work or Too Little Impact?," *Harvard Business Review*, December 10, 2021, https://hbr.org/2021/12/is-your-burnout-from-too-much-work-or-too-little-impact.

10. Aristotle notes, "The saying is attributed to both Theognis and Phocylides." Aristotle, *The Ethics of Aristotle: The Nicomachean Ethics*, trans. J. A. K. Thomson and Hugh Tredennick, rev. ed. (New York: Penguin Classics, 1976), 173.

11. David Brooks, *The Road to Character* (New York: Random House, 2015), 263.

12. Amy Peterson, *Where Goodness Still Grows: Reclaiming Virtue in an Age of Hypocrisy* (Nashville: Thomas Nelson, 2020), 114.

13. N. T. Wright, *After You Believe: Why Christian Character Matters* (New York: HarperOne, 2010), 27.

14. Rich Villodas (@richvillodas), Twitter post, March 29, 2022, 9:45 p.m., https://twitter.com/richvillodas/status/1508983724016345091.

15. In so many ways, our desire to form "good kids" reflects the dominance of "Moralistic Therapeutic Deism," a term coined by Christian Smith and his team during the groundbreaking National Study of Youth and Religion (NSYR). While the NSYR studied Millennials, the very notion of good kids reflects the lasting impact of Moralistic Therapeutic Deism on the church and Generation Z. This "de facto dominant religion" can be seen in the prevalence of five beliefs that form the "MTD creed": (1) God created, orders, and watches over the world; (2) God's desire is for people to be "good, nice, and fair" to each other; (3) God wants us to be "happy and to feel good about oneself"; (4) God is primarily needed to solve our problems; and (5) Good people go to heaven when they die. These beliefs are often embedded in what leaders and parents mean when they talk about good kids. See Christian Smith with Melinda Lundquist Denton, *Soul Searching: The Religious and Spiritual Lives of American Teenagers* (Oxford: Oxford University Press, 2005), 162–63.

16. Popularly attributed to Civil Rights leader John Lewis. Joe McCarthy, "10 John Lewis Quotes That Will Inspire You to Get Into 'Good Trouble,'" *Global Citizen*, July 20, 2020, https://www.globalcitizen.org/en/content/john-lewis-quotes/.

Chapter 2 Bare Spots and Bright Spots

1. Josephson Institute Center for Youth Ethics, "2012 Report Card on the Ethics of American Youth," accessed February 14, 2023, https://charactercounts.org/wp-content/uploads/2014/02/ReportCard-2012-DataTables.pdf, 11.

2. Michele Borba, *Thrivers: The Surprising Reasons Why Some Kids Struggle and Others Shine* (New York: Putnam, 2021), 141.

3. Borba, *Thrivers*, 141.

4. Christian Smith et al., *Lost in Transition: The Dark Side of Emerging Adulthood* (New York: Oxford University Press, 2011), 69.

5. Michael Levenson, "Lori Loughlin Begins 2-Month Sentence for Role in Admissions Scandal," *New York Times*, December 28, 2020, https://www.nytimes.com/2020/10/30/us/lori-loughlin-prison.html.

6. See Christian Smith with Melinda Lundquist Denton, *Soul Searching: The Religious and Spiritual Lives of American Teenagers* (New York: Oxford University Press, 2005), 57; and Kenda Creasy Dean, *Almost Christian: What the Faith of Our Teenagers Is Telling the American Church* (New York: Oxford University Press, 2010), 112ff.

7. Pew Research Center, "When Americans Say They Believe in God, What Do They Mean?," Pew Research Center, April 25, 2018, https://www.pewresearch.org/religion/2018/04/25/when-americans-say-they-believe-in-god-what-do-they-mean/.

8. David Briggs, "How Americans View God," *Faith and Leadership*, February 28, 2011, https://faithandleadership.com/how-americans-view-god.

9. Briggs, "How Americans View God."

10. Scot McKnight, "The Jesus We'll Never Know: Why scholarly attempts to discover the 'real' Jesus have failed. And why that's a good thing," *Christianity Today*, April 9, 2010, https://www.christianitytoday.com/ct/2010/april/15.22.html.

11. Gregory Boyle, *The Whole Language: The Power of Extravagant Tenderness* (New York: Avid Reader Press, 2021), 1.

12. James K. A. Smith, *You Are What You Love: The Spiritual Power of Habit* (Grand Rapids: Brazos, 2016), 146.

13. Jim Wilder and Michel Hendricks, *The Other Half of Church: Christian Community, Brain Science, and Overcoming Spiritual Stagnation* (Chicago: Moody, 2020), 24.

14. Brooks, *Road to Character*, 259.

15. Borba, *Thrivers*, 143.

16. Katelyn Beaty, *Celebrities for Jesus: How Personas, Platforms, and Profits Are Hurting the Church* (Grand Rapids: Brazos, 2022), 14.

17. Brooks, *Road to Character*, 6.

18. Borba, *Thrivers*, 143.

19. Determining chronological boundaries for generations is far from an exact or uniform scientific process. For example, Pew Research Forum defines *Millennials* as those born 1981–1996 and Gen Z as those born 1997–2012 (see Pew Research Center, "Defining Generations: Where Millennials End and Generation Z Begins," Pew Research Center, January 17, 2019, https://www.pewresearch.org/fact-tank/2019/01/17/where-millennials-end-and-generation-z-begins/). We've decided to round to years that are easier to remember.

20. We introduced these terms briefly in *3 Big Questions That Change Every Teenager* but have thoroughly updated our exploration given the dynamics of the last few years.

21. Health Resources and Services Administration's Maternal and Child Health Bureau, "Mental and Behavioral Health NSCH Data Brief," HRSA Maternal and Child Health, October 2020, https://mchb.hrsa.gov/sites/default /files/mchb/data-research/nsch-data-brief-2019-mental-bh.pdf.

22. Rajeev Ramchand, Joshua A. Gordon, and Jane L. Pearson, "Trends in Suicide Rates by Race and Ethnicity in the United States," *JAMA Network Open* 4, no. 5 (May 2021): e2111563, https://jamanetwork.com/journals/jama networkopen/fullarticle/2780380.

23. New York University, "Black Youth Suicide Rates Rising, Defying Historic Trends: Report," NYU news release, December 18, 2019, https://www.nyu.edu /about/news-publications/news/2019/december/BlackYouthSuicideRatesRising .html.

24. Ramchand, Gordon, and Pearson, "Trends in Suicide Rates by Race and Ethnicity."

25. Mark É. Czeisler et al., "Mental Health, Substance Use, and Suicidal Ideation During the COVID-19 Pandemic—United States, June 24–30, 2020," *Morbidity and Mortality Weekly Report* 69, no. 32 (August 14, 2020): 1049–57, https:// www.cdc.gov/mmwr/volumes/69/wr/mm6932a1.htm?s_cid=mm6932a1_w.

26. Kelsey Osgood, Hannah Sheldon-Dean, and Harry Kimball, "The Impact of the COVID-19 Pandemic on Children's Mental Health: What We Know So Far," *2021 Children's Mental Health Report*, https://childmind.org/wp-con tent/uploads/2021/10/CMHR-2021-FINAL.pdf, 8, 22.

27. Deborah M. Stone, Karin A. Mack, and Judith Qualters, "Notes from the Field: Recent Changes in Suicide Rates, by Race and Ethnicity and Age Group — United States, 2021," *Morbidity and Mortality Weekly Report* 72, no. 6 (February 10, 2023): 160–62, http://dx.doi.org/10.15585/mmwr.mm7206a4.

28. Centers for Disease Control and Prevention, *The Youth Risk Behavior Survey Data Summary & Trends Report: 2011–2021*, 59, https://www.cdc.gov /healthyyouth/data/yrbs/yrbs_data_summary_and_trends.htm.

29. STEER Education, "Girls' Mental Health 'At a Precipice' and Increasingly Worse than Boys', Data Shows," STEER Education, February 28, 2022, https://steer.education/girls-mental-health-at-a-precipice-and-increasingly -worse-than-boys-data-shows/.

30. Centers for Disease Control and Prevention, *The Youth Risk Behavior*, 2, 59.

31. Centers for Disease Control and Prevention, *The Youth Risk Behavior*, 2.

32. Springtide Research Institute, *The State of Religion and Young People 2022: Mental Health—What Faith Leaders Need to Know* (Winona, MN: Springtide Research Institute, 2022), 28–31.

33. Travis was part of a cohort of youth leaders trained by Indiana Wesleyan University.

34. Andrew Martin, "Adaptability Advantage: We Need More Than Just Resilience," Getting Smart, March 22, 2022, https://www.gettingsmart.com /2022/03/22/adaptability-advantage-we-need-more-than-just-resilience/.

35. Tracy Evans-Whipp and Constantine Gasser, "Adolescents' Resilience," chapter 10 in The Longitudinal Study of Australian Children, November 2019, https://growingupinaustralia.gov.au/research-findings/annual-statistical-re ports-2018/adolescents-resilience.

36. Louise Yarnall, "Promoting Grit, Tenacity, and Perseverance: Critical Factors for Success in the 21st Century," SRI International, November 1, 2018, https://www.sri.com/publication/education-learning-pubs/promoting-grit -tenacity-and-perseverance-critical-factors-for-success-in-the-21st-century/.

37. Evans-Whipp and Gasser, "Adolescents' Resilience."

38. Centers for Disease Control and Prevention, "Attention-Deficit / Hyper-activity Disorder (ADHD): Data and Statistics," Centers for Disease Control and Prevention, accessed February 14, 2023, https://www.cdc.gov/ncbddd/adhd /data.html.

39. Thirty-five percent of persons under eighteen years old fall under the 200 percent poverty threshold, categorized as "low income" or in poverty, as of 2021 estimates. Seventeen percent of persons under eighteen are in "deep poverty," under the 50 percent poverty threshold. United States Census Bureau, "POV01: Age and Sex of All People, Family Members and Unrelated Individuals: 2021," *Current Population Survey, 2022 Annual Social and Economic Supplement (CPS ASEC)*, https://www2.census.gov/programs-surveys/cps/tables/pov-01 /2022/pov01_200_1.xlsx.

40. Claudio O. Toppelberg and Brian A. Collins, "Language, Culture, and Adaptation in Immigrant Children," *Child and Adolescent Psychiatric Clinics of North America* 19, no. 4 (October 2010): 697–717, https://www.ncbi.nlm .nih.gov/pmc/articles/PMC3526379/; Edgar Demetrio Tovar-García, "The Impact of Perseverance and Passion for Long Term Goals (GRIT) on Educational Achievements of Migrant Children: Evidence from Tatarstan, Russia," *Psicología Educativa* 23, no. 1 (June 2017): 19–27, https://www.sciencedirect.com/science /article/pii/S1135755X17300040; Alejandro Portes and Alejandro Rivas, "The Adaptation of Migrant Children," *Future Child* 21, no. 1 (Spring 2011), https:// rhyclearinghouse.acf.hhs.gov/sites/default/files/docs/20068-The_Adaptation_of _Migrant.pdf.

41. John Joon-Young Huh, "Resilience in Asian American Adolescents: A Pastoral Theological Exploration of the Bicultural Self" (PhD diss., Princeton Theological Seminary, 2013), https://www.proquest.com/openview/9048ed 5571156a68732366957c98ac71/1?pq-origsite=gscholar&cbl=18750.

42. This story emerged from FYI's work in the Living a Better Story (LABS) Project, funded by a generous grant from Lilly Endowment Inc. and additional donors.

43. Nicholas Jones et al., "2020 Census Illuminates Racial and Ethnic Composition of the Country," United States Census Bureau, August 12, 2021, https://www.census.gov/library/stories/2021/08/improved-race-ethnicity -measures-reveal-united-states-population-much-more-multiracial.html.

44. Sabrina Tavernise and Robert Gebeloff, "Census Shows Sharply Growing Numbers of Hispanic, Asian and Multiracial Americans," *New York Times*,

August 12, 2021, https://www.nytimes.com/2021/08/12/us/us-census-population
-growth-diversity.html.

45. Jeffrey M. Jones, "LGBT Identification in U.S. Ticks Up to 7.1%," Gallup, February 17, 2022, https://news.gallup.com/poll/389792/lgbt-identification
-ticks-up.aspx.

46. Katherine Schaeffer, "As Schools Shift to Online Learning amid Pandemic, Here's What We Know about Disabled Students in the U.S.," Pew Research Center, April 23, 2020, https://www.pewresearch.org/fact-tank/2020/04
/23/as-schools-shift-to-online-learning-amid-pandemic-heres-what-we-know
-about-disabled-students-in-the-u-s/.

47. Springtide, "Spotify as a Religious Metaphor? (Yes, Go with It)," Springtide Research Institute, October 7, 2021, https://www.springtideresearch.org
/post/introducing-faith-unbundled.

48. Carey Nieuwhof, "7 Habits of Generation Z Your Church Might Be Ignoring," Carey Nieuwhof, accessed February 14, 2023, https://careynieuwhof.com
/7-habits-of-generation-z-that-your-church-might-be-ignoring/.

49. Amy's commitment to include diverse students was heightened by her participation in training from Flagler College.

50. Briggs, "How Americans View God."

Chapter 3 A New Compass

1. Special thanks to Tyler Greenway, FYI's research director for most of this project, for his leadership and expertise, as well as Aaron Yenney and Lisa Nopachai, whose time on our team focused exclusively on this grant-based project. Amy Carnall assisted tremendously in the final research steps and compiling stories for this book. Additional researchers included Miriam Cho, Quanesha Moore, Roslyn Hernández, Elizabeth Tamez Méndez, Levi Price, Yulee Lee, Jen Bradbury, Kara Powell, and Brad Griffin.

2. For a detailed analysis of this survey data, see Tyler S. Greenway et al., "'Many Are the Plans': An Analysis of Goals Described by Youth Ministry Leaders," *Archive for the Psychology of Religion*, vol 43, no. 3 (2021): 253–68, https://doi.org/10.1177/00846724211036965.

3. Interview analyses were conducted by Aaron Yenney, Miriam Cho, Lisa Nopachai, Quanesha Moore, Roslyn Hernández, Tyler Greenway, and Elizabeth Tamez Méndez. These analyses were led and synthesized by Jen Bradbury and Yulee Lee. Findings were then reviewed by additional FYI team members, including Kara Powell and Brad Griffin.

4. Lelac Almagor, "Whose Character? Why Character Education Is Inherently Flawed," *Boston Review*, November 26, 2013, https://bostonreview.net
/articles/lelac-almagor-character-education-inherent-flaws-schools/.

5. Miguel A. De La Torre, *Doing Christian Ethics from the Margins* (Maryknoll, NY: Orbis Books, 2014), 16.

6. Robert Chao Romero, *Brown Church: Five Centuries of Latina/o Social Justice, Theology, and Identity* (Downers Grove, IL: InterVarsity, 2020), 112.

7. Among the 378 survey participants, approximately 79.40 percent of the sample identified as White, 7.69 percent as Asian or Pacific Islander, 6.59 percent as Hispanic or Latino, 2.75 percent as Black or African American, 2.75 percent as Multiracial, 0.27 percent as Native American or American Indian, and 0.55 percent as other races or ethnicities.

8. Charles Taylor, *Sources of the Self* (Cambridge, MA: Harvard University Press, 1989), 27–28, 41.

Chapter 4 Cultivate Trust

1. Stephen M. R. Covey, *The Speed of Trust* (New York: Free Press, 2018), 1.

2. Ten percent of all respondents. Of the 1,491 Christian respondents in the study, the percentage was higher, but only by a smidge: 12 percent had heard from a faith leader. Springtide Research Institute, *The State of Religion and Young People 2021: Navigating Uncertainty* (Winona, MN: Springtide Research Institute, 2021), 22.

3. Springtide Research Institute, *State of Religion and Young People 2021*, 26.

4. Covey, *Speed of Trust*, 2.

5. "Secure relationships are more likely to develop when teachers are involved with, sensitive toward, and have frequent positive interactions with children." Christi Bergin and David Bergin, "Attachment in the Classroom," *Educational Psychological Review* 21 (2009): 154.

6. "Edelman Trust Barometer 2022," PowerPoint presentation, 2022, https://www.edelman.com/sites/g/files/aatuss191/files/2022-01/2022%20Edelman%20Trust%20Barometer%20FINAL_Jan25.pdf, 19.

7. "Edelman Trust Barometer 2022," 16.

8. Springtide Research Institute, *State of Religion and Young People 2021*, 33.

9. Springtide Research Institute, *State of Religion and Young People 2021*, 34.

10. Brené Brown, "The Anatomy of Trust," James Clear, accessed February 14, 2023, https://jamesclear.com/great-speeches/the-anatomy-of-trust-by-brene-brown.

11. Adapted from the "Emotional Bank Account" described by Stephen R. Covey, *The 7 Habits of Highly Effective People* (New York: Fireside, 1988), 188–90.

12. While we can't know for sure, it is likely that the disciples were older than age thirteen (which was typically the age a young man would start working full-time and/or leave home to follow a rabbi) and younger than age thirty (Jesus' age when he called the disciples to follow him; generally, disciples would be younger than their mentor).

13. "The Sermon on the Mount offers a profound insight into Jesus' social ethic and into his vision for discipleship and his people's life together. In Matthew 5:1–2 Jesus is surrounded by huge crowds. . . . Again, this isn't just a picture of the individual righteous life. This is a social ethic. This is a vision of a community of disciples who pursue lives together and in the world and who witness to him, to a new humanity, and to the age to come." Grace Ji-Sun Kim and Graham

Hill, *Healing Our Broken Humanity: Practices for Revitalizing the Church and Renewing the World* (Downers Grove, IL: InterVarsity, 2018), 152–53.

14. Our best sense of the disciples' fates is that James, the son of Zebedee, was executed by Herod (see Acts 12:2); Peter and Paul were martyred in AD 66 in Rome under Emperor Nero; Andrew was allegedly crucified after preaching in modern-day Russia, Turkey, and Greece; it is believed that Thomas was killed by the spears of four soldiers after he preached the gospel in India; Matthew might not have been martyred, but if he was, it was likely via a stabbing in Ethiopia; after converting the wife of a Roman proconsul in Asia Minor, Philip was put to death; Bartholomew was an active missionary to India, Armenia, and Ethiopia, with multiple differing accounts of how he was killed; the Jewish historian Josephus reported that James was stoned and then clubbed to death; Simon the Zealot ministered in Persia and was killed when he refused to worship a sun god; Matthias was burned to death in Syria; and Judas Iscariot hung himself following his betrayal of Jesus (Matt. 27:5). It is quite possible that John, the author of the book of Revelation, is the only disciple who died from natural causes after being exiled to the island of Patmos.

15. This definition and the following insights are derived largely from the work of M. H. Davis, *Empathy: A Social Psychological Approach* (New York: Routledge, 1994) and explained further in Kara Powell and Brad M. Griffin, *3 Big Questions That Change Every Teenager: Making the Most of Your Conversations and Connections* (Grand Rapids: Baker Books, 2021), 52–63.

16. Adapted from former Fuller Seminary professor David W. Augsburger, *Caring Enough to Hear and Be Heard* (Ventura, CA: Regal Books, 1982), 12.

Chapter 5 Model Growth

1. The University of Birmingham (UK) Jubilee Centre for Character and Virtues has popularized the phrase "character caught, character taught, character sought" in its framework. See "The Character Teaching Inventory" at https://www.jubileecentre.ac.uk/2955/character-education/teacher-resources. Further, it is well established in parenting research that parents need to not only use parenting strategies that foster specific character outcomes but also model those outcomes. The same is true for educators. See Marvin W. Berkowitz, Melinda C. Bier, and B. McCauley, "Toward a Science of Character Education," *Journal of Character Education* 13, no. 1 (2017): 44–45.

2. The term *role model* was coined by sociologist Robert K. Merton, popularized in the 1970s–1990s.

3. See Marian Wright Edelman, "It's Hard to Be What You Can't See," Children's Defense Fund, August 21, 2015, https://www.childrensdefense.org/child-watch-columns/health/2015/its-hard-to-be-what-you-cant-see/.

4. The peak in percentage of women serving in pastoral positions was 12.2 percent in 1925; this dropped to its lowest point of 1.1 percent in 1985 and raised slightly to 3.7 percent by 2003. Richard Houseal, "Nazarene Clergy Women: A Statistical Analysis from 1908–2003" (presented at the Association of Nazarene Sociologists and Researchers Annual Conference, 2003), 4, 10.

5. Michael Barbaro, "A Coal Miner's Political Transformation," *The Daily* (podcast), August 22, 2022, https://www.nytimes.com/2022/08/22/podcasts/the -daily/alabama-coal-mine-strike.html?.

6. See Kara Powell, Cheryl Crawford, and Brad M. Griffin, *Sticky Faith, Youth Worker Edition: Practical Ideas to Nurture Long-Term Faith in Teenagers* (Grand Rapids: Zondervan, 2011).

7. See Kara Powell, Jake Mulder, and Brad M. Griffin, *Growing Young: 6 Essential Strategies to Help Young People Discover and Love Your Church* (Grand Rapids: Baker Books, 2016).

8. "We have created youth ministry that confuses extroversion with faithfulness. . . . If we effectively communicate to young people that being a serious follower of Jesus is synonymous with being an extrovert for Jesus, then all of our young people who simply are not wired that way are going to quietly assume they can't be Christians." James K. A. Smith, *You Are What You Love*, 147.

9. Mark DeVries, *Sustainable Youth Ministry: Why Most Youth Ministry Doesn't Last and What Your Church Can Do about It* (Downers Grove, IL: InterVarsity, 2008), 42–44.

10. Across six different studies, extroverts were judged to be worse listeners by interaction partners. Researchers found a significant negative correlation between extroversion and perceived listening. Francis J. Flynn, Hanne Collins, and Julian Zlatev, "Are You Listening to Me? The Negative Link Between Extraversion and Perceived Listening," *Personality and Social Psychology Bulletin*, advance online publication, March 18, 2022, https://doi.org/10.1177/014 61672211072815.

11. Susan Cain, *Quiet: The Power of Introverts in a World That Can't Stop Talking* (New York: Crown Publishing Group, 2012).

12. Henri Nouwen, *The Selfless Way of Christ: Downward Mobility and the Spiritual Life* (Maryknoll, NY: Orbis Books, 2011).

13. Diana Butler Bass, *Freeing Jesus: Rediscovering Jesus as Friend, Teacher, Savior, Lord, Way, and Presence* (New York: HarperOne, 2021), 61.

14. "The disciples were called Christians first at Antioch" (Acts 11:26). The Greek is Χριστιανός, or "little Christ," "followers of Christ." *Thayer's Greek Lexicon*, s.v. "Strong's G5546," electronic database (Biblesoft, Inc., 2002, 2003, 2006, 2011).

15. Giovanny Panginda, "Models Matter: Key Insights on Character-Forming Discipleship with Teenagers," Fuller Youth Institute, July 5, 2022, https://fuller youthinstitute.org/blog/models-matter.

16. Panginda, "Models Matter."

17. Thomas Merton, *Seeds of Contemplation* (Norfolk, CT: New Directions, 1949), 66.

18. The emerging term *Latine* is used here in place of Latina/o/x to promote inclusivity and to highlight the diversity of the Latina/o experience and background in self-identification, ethnicity, culture, gender, sexuality, place of birth, primary language use, and so forth, and as a term that better aligns with Spanish linguistic roots.

Chapter 6 Teach for Transformation

1. Saga Briggs, "The Science of Attention: How to Capture and Hold the Attention of Easily Distracted Students," informED, June 28, 2014, https://www.open colleges.edu.au/informed/features/30-tricks-for-capturing-students-attention/.

2. Aleszu Bajak, "Lectures Aren't Just Boring, They're Ineffective, Too, Study Finds," *Science*, May 12, 2014, https://www.science.org/content/article/lectures -arent-just-boring-theyre-ineffective-too-study-finds.

3. Stanley Hauerwas, *State of the University* (Oxford: Wiley, 2007), 46.

4. This point about advertent or inadvertent character education has been widely explored in the field of education research. See Henry F. Algera and Christopher A. Sink, "Another Look at Character Education in Christian Schools," *Journal of Research on Christian Education* 11, no. 2 (2002): 161–81; Thomas Lickona, *Educating for Character: How Our Schools Can Teach Respect and Responsibility* (New York: Bantam, 1992); Marvin W. Berkowitz, *Parenting for Good: Real World Advice for Parents from the Character Columns of Dr. Marvin W. Berkowitz* (Greensboro, NC: Character Development Group, 2005).

5. Dallas Willard, *Renovation of the Heart: Putting On the Character of Christ* (Colorado Springs: NavPress, 2002), 238.

6. Borba, *Thrivers*, 151.

7. Borba, *Thrivers*, 151.

8. Bass, *Freeing Jesus*, 30.

9. Bass, *Freeing Jesus*, 43.

10. Bass, *Freeing Jesus*, 44.

11. Martin B. Copenhaver, *Jesus Is the Question: The 307 Questions Jesus Asked and the 3 He Answered* (Nashville: Abingdon, 2014), xix.

12. Copenhaver, *Jesus Is the Question*, xix.

13. Amanda Hontz Drury, *Saying Is Believing: The Necessity of Testimony in Adolescent Spiritual Development* (Downers Grove, IL: IVP Academic, 2015), 15.

14. Drury, *Saying Is Believing*, 15.

15. Borba, *Thrivers*, 151.

16. An interviewee quoting an image widely attributed to business researcher Jim Collins, first published in *Good to Great: Why Some Companies Make the Leap . . . and Others Don't* (New York: HarperBusiness, 2001).

Chapter 7 Practice Together

1. Andrew Root, *Revisiting Relational Youth Ministry: From a Strategy of Influence to a Theology of Incarnation* (Downers Grove, IL: InterVarsity, 2007).

2. Dorothy Bass, *Way to Live: Christian Practices for Teens* (Nashville: Upper Room Books, 2002), 292.

3. Carrie Doehring, "Searching for Wholeness amidst Traumatic Grief: The Role of Spiritual Practices That Reveal Compassion in Embodied, Relational, and Transcendent Ways," *Pastoral Psychology* 68, no. 3 (2019): 241–59.

4. Bessel van der Kolk, *The Body Keeps the Score: Brain, Mind, and Body in the Healing of Trauma* (New York: Viking, 2014).

5. By *intersectional*, we mean the interconnected nature of social categories such as race, class, and gender that can be experienced by an individual or group. The term was originally coined by Black feminist scholar Kimberlé Williams Crenshaw, cofounder of the African American Policy Forum, and has come to be used widely across many disciplines, including practical theology.

6. Smith, *You Are What You Love*, 153.

7. Smith, *You Are What You Love*, 153.

8. For a thorough treatment of this idea, see Henri J. M. Nouwen, *The Wounded Healer: Ministry in Contemporary Society* (New York: Image, 1979).

9. Boyle, *Whole Language*, 24, 28.

10. For practical ideas about how to practice lament in youth ministry, see the two-part blog series by Caleb Roose, "Helping Young People Process Anger and Grief through Lament," Fuller Youth Institute, June 9, 2022, https://fuller youthinstitute.org/blog/helping-young-people-process-anger-and-grief-through -lament.

11. Kenneth I. Pargament, Serena Wong, and Julie J. Exline, "Wholeness and Holiness: The Spiritual Dimension of Eudaimonics," in *The Handbook of Eudaimonic Well-Being*, ed. Joar Vittersø (Switzerland: Springer International, 2016), 379–94.

12. LGBTQ+ identity further amplifies the likelihood of ACEs. See Philip M. Hughes et al., "Adverse Childhood Experiences Across Birth Generation and LGBTQ+ Identity, Behavioral Risk Factor Surveillance System, 2019," *American Journal of Public Health* 112, no. 4 (April 2022): 662–70, https://doi.org/10 .2105/AJPH.2021.306642.

Chapter 8 Make Meaning

1. "Søren Kierkegaard Quotes," BrainyQuote, accessed September 19, 2022, https://www.brainyquote.com/quotes/soren_kierkegaard_105030.

2. Scott Cormode, "Multi-Layered Leadership: The Christian Leader as Builder, Shepherd, and Gardener," *Journal of Religious Leadership* 1, no. 2 (Fall 2002): 71.

3. Special thanks to Lisa Nopachai for this reflection.

4. Pamela Ebstyne King, Susan Mangan, and Rodrigo Riveros, "Religion, Spirituality, and Youth Thriving: Investigating the Roles of the Developing Mind and Meaning-Making," in *Handbook of Positive Psychology, Religion, and Spirituality*, ed. Edward B. Davis, Everett L. Worthington Jr., and Sarah A. Schnitker (New York: Springer, 2022), 271.

5. Powell and Griffin, *3 Big Questions That Change Every Teenager*, 148.

6. Technology use is part of this story, but we want to be careful not to villainize it (or young people for navigating their digital worlds). Researchers are finding that increased technology use has shifted the way we think, decreasing sustained cognition and increasing distractibility. See Joseph Firth et al., "The 'Online Brain': How the Internet May Be Changing Our Cognition," *World Psychiatry* 18, no. 2 (2019): 119–29, https://doi.org/10.1002/wps.20617.

7. Research in neuroscience has linked morality, social flexibility, empathy, and complex thinking to the ventral prefrontal cortex, a part of the brain that

develops slowly throughout adolescence and young adulthood. Adolescents, therefore, are still developing the mental ability to make meaning from complex, abstract, or emotional experiences. See Eric E. Nelson and Amanda E. Guyer, "The Development of the Ventral Prefrontal Cortex and Social Flexibility," *Developmental Cognitive Neuroscience* 1, no. 3 (2011): 233–45, https://doi.org /10.1016/j.dcn.2011.01.002; Leo Pascual, Paulo Rodrigues, and David Gallardo-Pujol, "How Does Morality Work in the Brain? A Functional and Structural Perspective of Moral Behavior," *Frontiers in Integrative Neuroscience* 7 (2013): 65, https://doi.org/10.3389/fnint.2013.00065.

8. Andrew Root, *Faith Formation in a Secular Age: Responding to the Church's Obsession with Youthfulness* (Grand Rapids: Baker Academic, 2017), 145–46.

9. Simon Sinek has made much of this in his work. See Simon Sinek, *Start with Why: How Great Leaders Inspire Everyone to Take Action* (New York: Portfolio, 2009).

10. Susan David, *Emotional Agility: Get Unstuck, Embrace Change, and Thrive in Work and Life* (New York: Avery, 2016), 121.

11. David, *Emotional Agility*, 117.

12. Adapted from David, *Emotional Agility*, 118.

13. Kate Bowler, *No Cure for Being Human: (And Other Truths I Need to Hear)* (New York: Random House, 2021), 183.

14. Published originally as Kara E. Powell and Brad M. Griffin, *Deep Justice Journeys Leader's Guide* (Grand Rapids: Zondervan, 2009), and later revised and re-released as *Sticky Faith Service Guide: Moving Students from Mission Trips to Missional Living* (Grand Rapids: Zondervan, 2016). The model behind this process is adapted from the experiential education framework originally proposed by Laura Joplin and later modified and tested by Terry Linhart. In the center of the model is a cycle (Joplin pictured it as a hurricane) of challenging experience paired with reflection. See Laura Joplin, "On Defining Experiential Education," *Journal of Experiential Education* 4, no. 1 (1981): 17–20; Terry Linhart, "Planting Seeds: The Curricular Hope of Short Term Mission Experiences in Youth Ministry," *Christian Education Journal* 2, no. 2 (2005): 256–72, https://doi.org/10.1177/073989130500200203.

15. This maxim is attributed to John Dewey but is likely a paraphrase. See Robert Lagueux, "A Spurious John Dewey Quotation on Reflection," Berklee College of Music, accessed September 19, 2022, https://www.academia.edu /17358587/A_Spurious_John_Dewey_Quotation_on_Reflection.

16. Almeda M. Wright, *The Spiritual Lives of Young African Americans* (New York: Oxford University Press, 2017), 214, emphasis in original.

Chapter 9 Your Own Map

1. Anne Snyder, *The Fabric of Character: A Wise Giver's Guide to Supporting Social and Moral Renewal* (Washington, DC: Philanthropy Roundtable, 2019), 10.

2. Max De Pree, *Leadership Is an Art* (New York: Currency Doubleday, 1989), 9.

KARA POWELL, PHD,

is the chief of leadership formation and executive director of the Fuller Youth Institute (FYI) at Fuller Theological Seminary (see FullerYouthInstitute .org). Named by *Christianity Today* as one of "50 Women to Watch," Kara serves as a youth and family strategist for Orange and speaks regularly at parenting and leadership conferences. Kara has authored or coauthored numerous books, including *3 Big Questions That Shape Your Future*, *3 Big Questions That Change Every Teenager*, *Growing With*, *Growing Young*, *The Sticky Faith Guide for Your Family*, and the entire Sticky Faith series. Kara and her husband, Dave, are regularly inspired by the learning and laughter that come from their three teenage and young adult children.

Connect with Kara:

KaraPowell.com

 @Kara.Powell.Author

 @KPowellFYI

 @KPowellFYI

JEN BRADBURY

serves as the content director for the Fuller Youth Institute and a volunteer youth pastor at her local church. With more than twenty years of experience in youth ministry, she's the author of several books, including *The Jesus*

Gap, The Real Jesus, Called: A Novel About Youth Ministry Transition, and *What Do I Believe About What I Believe?* Jen and her husband, Doug, live in the Chicagoland area, where they can regularly be found adventuring with their two young daughters.

Connect with Jen:

YMJen.com

 @Jen.Bradbury.7

 @YMJen

@YMJen

BRAD M. GRIFFIN

is the senior director of content and research for the Fuller Youth Institute, where he develops research-based resources for youth ministry leaders and families. A speaker, writer, and volunteer pastor, Brad is the coauthor of over fifteen books, including *3 Big Questions That Shape Your Future*, *3 Big Questions That Change Every Teenager*, *Growing Young*, and several Sticky Faith books. Brad and his wife, Missy, live in Southern California and share life with their three teenage and young adult children.

Connect with Brad:

FullerYouthInstitute.org

 @Brad.Griffin

 @BGriffinFYI